Cybersecurity Training

Cybersecurity Training

A Pathway to Readiness

Gregory J. Skulmoski and Chris Walker

BEP

BUSINESS EXPERT PRESS

Leader in applied, concise business books

Cybersecurity Training: A Pathway to Readiness

Cover design by Gregory J. Skulmoski

Photo courtesy of Pexels.com, (*Laptop Over A White Desk*, Anna Nekrashevich)

Interior design by Exeter Premedia Services Private Ltd., Chennai, India

First published in 2023 by
Business Expert Press, LLC
222 East 46th Street, New York, NY 10017
www.businessexpertpress.com

ISBN-13: 978-1-63742-553-4 (paperback)
ISBN-13: 978-1-63742-554-1 (e-book)

Business Expert Press Portfolio and Project Management Collection

First edition: 2023

Description

Organizations face increasing cybersecurity attacks that threaten their sensitive data, systems, and existence, but there are solutions. Experts recommend cybersecurity training and general awareness learning experiences as strategic necessities; however, organizations lack cybersecurity training planning, implementation, and optimization guidance. *Cybersecurity Training: A Pathway to Readiness* addresses the demand to provide cybersecurity training aligned with the normal flow of IT project delivery and technology operations.

Cybersecurity Training combines best practices found in standards and frameworks like ITIL technology management, NIST Cybersecurity Framework, ISO risk, quality and information security management systems, and the *Guide to the Project Management Body of Knowledge.* Trainers will appreciate the approach that builds on the ADDIE Model of Instructional Design, Bloom's Taxonomy of Cognitive Thought, and Kirkpatrick's Model of Evaluation, a trilogy of training best practices.

Readers learn to apply this proven project-oriented training approach to improve the probability of successful cybersecurity awareness and role-based training experiences. The reader is guided to initiate, plan, design, develop, pilot, implement, and evaluate training and learning, followed by continual improvement sprints and projects.

Cybersecurity Training prepares trainers, project managers, and IT security professionals to deliver and optimize cybersecurity training so that organizations and its people are ready to prevent and mitigate cybersecurity threats, leading to more resilient organizations.

Keywords

NIST cybersecurity awareness and role-based training; specialized cybersecurity training; ADDIE Model of Instructional Design; Bloom's Taxonomy; Kirkpatrick's Model of Evaluation; project-oriented cybersecurity training; cybersecurity readiness; ITIL technology management; cybersecurity resilience; Lean Six Sigma; agile project management; quantum cybersecurity

Contents

Testimonials

Cybersecurity Training: A Pathway to Readiness was peer-reviewed by a diverse group of project management, instructional designers, and cybersecurity practitioners. Our peer review sample of experts was heterogenous, representing project management, instructional design, and cybersecurity. Fifteen subject matter experts were invited to participate in a peer review process, and nine reviewed *Cybersecurity Training* and returned constructive comments, recommendations for change, and praise. The project management reviewers deliver today's innovations on time, on budget, and to the delight of their customers. The cybersecurity reviewers are on the leading edge of protecting organizations and understand where cybersecurity is evolving and needs to mature. Finally, instructional design specialists reviewed *Cybersecurity Training* and gave guidance about our project-oriented approach to cybersecurity training.

We thank our reviewers like Derek Molnar, Thomas Edgerton, and others like Irene Corpuz, who gave praise and constructive criticism like only a seasoned cybersecurity specialist can: "One area to improve would be to provide a more context on why ISO/IEC 27001 and NIST Cybersecurity Framework are important for organizations to follow (i.e., when would it be advisable to implement NIST over ISO/IEC 27001, and vice-versa)." The personal pronoun "we" is being used to refer to the authors of *Cybersecurity Training*. We incorporated Irene's and other peer reviewers' feedback, which strengthened our book. Thank you again!

"Highly recommended"

"Cybersecurity readiness is becoming increasingly critical as people remain the weakest link despite the widely available information on the Internet about massive attacks caused by a single end user clicking on a 'click-bait' link (i.e., phishing e-mail). But what is wrong with the ongoing cybersecurity awareness training the organizations offer their employees? Were they designed strategically according to specific training models? Were they executed correctly and treated as a project?

Cybersecurity is often seen as a technical responsibility, but in the book Cybersecurity Training: A Pathway to Readiness, *authors Greg and Chris encourage readers to merge strategic thinking and project management when implementing a cybersecurity readiness program. They discuss creating a cybersecurity awareness culture aligned with the organization's vision, principles, goals, and objectives. Doing so provides a 'learning ecosystem that encourages life-long and ubiquitous learning,' supporting the organization's cybersecurity-related KPIs. It also discusses combining the training ecosystem's tailoring and principles to achieve the most beneficial delivery plan.*

Thus, Cybersecurity Training *is highly recommended for project managers, the HR training section, and the cybersecurity readiness team."*—**Irene Corpuz, United Arab Emirates, MSc, CISA, ISO 27k Lead Auditor and Lead Implementer, ITIL, PMP, PMI-ACP, Co-Founder and Board Member—Women in Cyber Security Middle East, Global Advisory Board Member—EC Council**

"A to Z in cybersecurity training"

"I'm very impressed with the overall cybersecurity training model beautifully detailed in Cybersecurity Training: A Pathway to Readiness. *I can use these techniques; if the reader follows this approach that combines best practices from training, project management, and relevant standards, they will remove most project risks. Chris and Greg have written an easy-to-read book that guides the reader to plan and implement cybersecurity training by removing guesswork and leaving no room for errors. They have captured everything from A to Z in cybersecurity training."*—**Zaid Al Ardah, Director, Technical Protective Operations, Cleveland Clinic, United States**

"An incredible book that empowered and inspired me"

*"*Cybersecurity Training *is an incredible book that empowered and inspired me. The authors, Greg and Chris, write with a genuine passion for cybersecurity readiness and its critical role in the success and survival of organizations.*

Their writing is characterized by a deep knowledge of the subject matter, evident in the comprehensive overview of NIST cybersecurity functions and the Goldilocks Approach to cybersecurity. The authors stress the importance of a holistic approach to cybersecurity readiness involving people, processes, and technologies. Cybersecurity Training *emphasizes the importance of seeing cybersecurity frameworks as a guide rather than a rigid set of rules. By doing so, organizations can balance cybersecurity with business objectives and avoid unnecessary constraints on their partners.*

What impressed me most about the book was the authors' unwavering belief that cybersecurity readiness is everyone's responsibility. Their call to action for organizations to shift toward designing-in cybersecurity as a routine matter is bold and inspiring. I was particularly moved by their invitation to business partners from the finance and supply chain departments to join to improve resilience.

Overall, Cybersecurity Training *is an excellent book written with character and passion. It inspired me to act and make a difference in the fight against cyber threats."*—**Charles Aunger, CEO/President/Founder, HEAL Security Inc., United States**

"A timely and innovative approach"

*"*Cybersecurity Training *provides an innovative holistic project management approach that combines the best practices of established instructional design, training, and learning programs (e.g., ADDIE, Bloom's Taxonomy, and Kirkpatrick). This blueprint will guide your organization as it builds a resilient cybersecurity operation. I congratulate Chris and Greg for their timely and innovative approach to cybersecurity training. Fantastic!"* **—Rhoda DiCrescenzo, CCNA, CCNI, Sr. eLearning Specialist and Instructional Designer and Trainer, United States**

"The first worldwide reference"

"According to IIBA and IEEE Computer Society, a hacker attack occurs every 39 seconds. Also, according to the 2022 (ISC)^2 Cybersecurity Workforce Study, there's a global shortage of 3.4 million cybersecurity-related jobs. This could signal that society needs to change its thoughts about cybersecurity and invite nontechnical participants to join cybersecurity teams. The first building block, 'a well-thought cybersecurity awareness program,' is the starting point. Greg and Chris's book proves this can be successfully achieved.

As a business analyst, program manager, and professional trainer for over 20 years, I have found this book to be the first worldwide reference combining cybersecurity, project management, and training with a ready-to-action perspective. Read it, study it, and tailor it to your specific context. Get ready now to help your organization proactively manage cybersecurity risks."—**Rafa Pagán MSc, CBAP, CPOA, AAC, PMP, PMI-ACP, PMI-PBA, PMI-RMP, PMI-SP, OPEN PM2, KANBAN, POWER BI, MCTS, MCITP, CTT+, SAMC, SDC, SMC, SPOC, SSMC, SSPOC, CSM, CSPO, PSM, PSPO, COMPTIA, Freelance Consultant and Trainer, Madrid, Spain**

"Invaluable resource for both beginners and experts"

"As the CEO of a management consulting company that delivers innovation through projects, cybersecurity has increasingly gained attention in the last 15 years of my consultancy. Unfortunately, and more often than not, there is a disconnect among project team members as they are grounded in their own discipline's tradition, culture, and language. A disconnected project team is not a recipe for project success. Skulmoski and Walker, in Cybersecurity Training: A Pathway to Readiness, *have aligned cybersecurity training and project management with global standards, frameworks, and best practices, resulting in an invaluable resource for beginners and experts."*—**Dr.-Ing. Alexander Lang, CEO IMAN Solutions GmbH, Munich, Germany**

"A hands-on guide to cybersecurity training"

"Skulmoski and Walker take the complex IT and educational frameworks that guide modern organizations and meld them into an approachable guide to cybersecurity training focusing on delivering successful projects that provide true value to organizations.

The design of Cybersecurity Training *makes it a perfect guide for anyone looking to educate themselves on the current approaches within IT and education and how to blend both to deliver value.*

For educators, Cybersecurity Training, *with its comprehensive yet approachable guides to IT and educational frameworks, paired with microlearning sections, enhances and invites the reader to explore key concepts. The authors provide a perfect reference for students on delivering value by utilizing proven project management and training best practices."*—**Derek Molnar PMP, IT Project Manager, Colorado State University, United States**

Foreword

Chris Walker and I met at the beginning of the Cleveland Clinic Abu Dhabi hospital project, where I was on the owner's side and Chris on the vendor's side. Our project was to train approximately 3,500 caregivers representing 550 positions ranging from surgeons, accountants, phlebotomists, pharmacy technicians, respiratory nurses, registration specialists, and many more. I was assigned the training project due to my background (e.g., a university professor with a Bachelor of Education degree and a Canadian professional teaching license). Our CIO asked me to review the training contract before our organization signed the document.

The next day, the CIO asked me what I thought, and I responded, "This contract is for training. We don't want training; we want learning." We then examined training as an input and the vendor could provide double the number of contracted training hours, and our organization still might not have competent systems users. However, if we signed a contract based on outputs (e.g., learning outcomes), our training project team could track learning KPIs. Indeed, the vendor could achieve the contracted KPIs and underspend with a lean approach. The vendor liked this innovative approach to training, and a training contract was signed where training continued until 80 percent of our caregivers received an average mark of 80 percent on assessments. The assessments were developed in collaboration with the business units to ensure that proper learning occurred and was assessed.

Chris arranged and led a highly skilled training team, and we provided training to our caregivers as outlined in this book. Training in the Middle East and for specialized skillsets required for a first-class hospital brings unique risks, such as unpredictable new caregiver arrivals due to at-home work obligations and visa approval time variances. We used risk management and other project management approaches to deliver training successfully. Our project team trained 90 percent of our caregivers, who earned an average of 90 percent on their assessments. Our vendor, led by Chris, delivered a successful training project, came in under budget, and the Cleveland Clinic Abu Dhabi hospital was safely opened with competent caregivers.

Fundamental to *Cybersecurity Training* is the authors ("we") rely on best practices in project management, risk and quality management, and training. We are aware that no one model fits all training circumstances. "As you begin your study of instructional design, bear in mind that models of instructional design/development are helpful guides to the process, but no single model should be considered a lock-step recipe for creating instruction, nor is any one model the only correct way to design instruction" (Brown and Green 2016, 12). Project managers "tailor" tools and processes to the unique project context. Therefore, we invite you to tailor our instructional design models, standards, and frameworks to your projects to improve the probability of success.

Our book is structured in three parts. In PART I, we review the burgeoning demand for cybersecurity training. Simply, the demand for cybersecurity training is increasing because there is an increase in cybersecurity incidents, with the expectation that the need for cybersecurity readiness will continue for years to come. The main drivers include waves of digital transformation; a recent wave of digital transformation was triggered by the COVID-19 pandemic, resulting in the massive adoption of technologies to support new ways of working. Unfortunately, cybersecurity was not always a high priority, resulting in many vulnerabilities, attacks, and the increased need for cybersecurity training. The following digital transformation wave features AI-embedded functionalities where organizations launch new projects to implement and protect these new systems, leading to an increased demand for training. Finally, quantum computing will enhance or displace AI-based systems, resulting in new projects and training. Government regulatory bodies and insurance companies are responding with more cybersecurity regulations and cybersecurity readiness expectations for reduced cybersecurity premiums. Thus, there is an increased and sustained demand for cybersecurity training.

PART I continues with an overview of globally recognized training and education models and frameworks that *Cybersecurity Training* incorporates: the ADDIE (Analyze, Design, Develop, Implement, and Evaluate) Model of Instructional Design, Bloom's Taxonomy of Cognitive

Thought, and the Kirkpatrick Model of Evaluation. These training best practices are longstanding and successful that can be used in cybersecurity training. In PART I, we align our training with the Information Technology Infrastructure Library (ITIL) framework. The ITIL framework guides organizations to plan, deliver, and optimize digital products (e.g., new laptops, printers, servers, etc.) and services (e.g., e-mail, human resource information systems, pharmacy systems, IT, etc.).

We review the National Institute of Standards (NIST) Cybersecurity Framework in PART I. The NIST Cybersecurity Framework includes a comprehensive suite of documents to guide organizations to provide cybersecurity, including the (1) identify, (2) protect, (3) detect, (4) respond, (5) recover, and (6) govern functions. Cybersecurity training can optimize these six functions to achieve cybersecurity readiness. The NIST Cybersecurity Framework is widely adopted globally in over 100 countries and translated into 10 languages, including English, Arabic, Japanese, Spanish, Portuguese, and Polish, with more translations promised. Therefore, in *Cybersecurity Training*, we align with the generally accepted NIST Cybersecurity Framework and supporting documents.

Finally, in PART I, we use the hybrid project delivery approach to deliver technologies, products, and services like cybersecurity. We align the ITIL framework, NIST Cybersecurity Framework,[1] and project management with the ADDIE Model of Instructional Design to improve the probability of successful cybersecurity training. These models and frameworks are incorporated into an adaptive learning ecosystem to help achieve cybersecurity readiness. Therefore, we combine previously disconnected best practices into a holistic approach to deliver cybersecurity training, a critical success factor for organizational readiness and resilience.

In PART II, we apply the ADDIE Model of Instructional Design phases to cybersecurity training using a project management delivery approach. We use the same project management approach to deliver and optimize NIST Cybersecurity Framework aligned training: general security awareness and specialized (role-based) cybersecurity training. Thus, we align best practices to deliver and optimize training, including

---

[1] The reader will benefit from downloading and reviewing the NIST documents as we introduce them in this book.

ongoing learning experiences to achieve cybersecurity readiness. Combining best practices, standards, and frameworks helps achieve the desired training quality while keeping risks low.

This book is written for those who strive to deliver, maintain, and optimize cybersecurity readiness, particularly subject matter experts from project management, IT security, and instructional design. The IT security reader will recognize their best practices when cybersecurity is discussed and may find new content in the project management and instructional design sections. The instructional designer may be more interested in project management and cybersecurity than instructional design content. Likewise, the project manager may spend more time with the cybersecurity and instructional design sections rather than the project management sections, but all readers will appreciate how all are aligned. Thus, we have a diverse audience in *Cybersecurity Training*, and we provide an integrated approach to cybersecurity readiness by improving the capabilities of an organization's people.

Finally, we include appendixes in PART III, including a leaderboard use case. Educators increasingly use gamification techniques like leaderboards to improve learner engagement, leading to improved learning outcome achievements. Other appendixes include a glossary and an instructional design team overview.

We include microlearning opportunities where we guide the reader to online resources to learn more about concepts presented in *Cybersecurity Training*. We take a unique approach to learning where the reader will benefit from both end-to-end readings and a focused approach to reviewing concepts that you might want to use in your live projects, including near-term quantum technologies projects. Thus, this book is a learning resource you can reuse to improve the probability of training success.

Acknowledgments

I worked in Finance crunching numbers, and one day, my boss asked me to purchase twelve 386SX computers as part of the annual capital budgeting cycle: my first "IT project." Later, I participated in the selection team for a new financial system. Our project team implemented a customized system that was late and over budget. I wanted to learn more about business to become better at projects, and I completed a traditional MBA. Even with this new business knowledge about labor law, return on investment calculations, and the four pillars of marketing, my projects continued to struggle. I searched for answers and discovered the project management specialty.

I enrolled in a project management program at the University of Calgary and learned how to plan and implement projects. Many passionate teachers taught me the tools, processes, and finer points of project management (and teaching). Thank you, Professors Francis Hartman, George Jergeas, Janice Thomas, and Mr. Ken Hanley. All had practical project experience, which helped me tailor my project management approach. Dr. Francis Hartman led the project management specialization program and brought together engaged students to learn and have fun while polishing their assignments. I also met forward thinkers like John Paiaro, owner of Stream Data Systems, who leads and succeeds with project management best practices. Very quickly, it seemed that I was almost finished with my dissertation and thinking about what to do next. I spoke with Francis, and he recommended working in the Middle East. Shortly after that, I was hired by Zayed University in Abu Dhabi, United Arab Emirates, to teach project management. No one has taught me more about projects than Francis. Thank you. RIP.

I taught project management at the College of Information Technology for nine years, enjoyed academia, and saw our students learn, graduate, and lead. However, I yearned to practice what I professed and manage projects. I left Zayed University and joined Cleveland Clinic Abu Dhabi as a project manager near the beginning of the project. I delivered

14 strategic projects ranging from technical (e.g., IoT through to cloud technologies) to nontechnical projects (e.g., internal auditing, including cybersecurity standards compliance).

I worked in a PMO (Project Management Office) that tailored and combined leading standards such as ITIL, ISO/IEC 27000:2018 Information Security Management, ISO 9001 Quality Management, the PMBOK® Guide, and other globally accepted health care-related standards. I experienced how aligning standards and frameworks can help to deliver projects on time, on budget, and to the correct and exacting levels of quality required in health care. I learned from my leadership (both technical and clinical), and I am grateful for the collegiality of my colleagues and team members. The tools, processes, and techniques in this book were implemented and refined, delivering projects at Cleveland Clinic Abu Dhabi. I was fortunate to win the 2017 Middle East Security Award, Chief Information Security Officers Council—*100 Rising Stars in Security and Risk* for how I managed risks in technology and training projects: hybrid project delivery works. After seven years leading on the sharp end of projects, I returned to academia and joined the project innovation management program at Bond University, Australia.

I enjoyed being back in the classroom with diverse project experiences to share with our students. My students are a source of influence: they graduate, work, and often contact me with their stories of successfully applying the techniques in my previous book, *Shields Up: A Project Management Approach to Cybersecurity*. I am grateful to Dr. Kam Jugdev and the BEP Collection Editor, Dr. Timothy J. Kloppenborg, for their guidance in writing these project management books. The BEP publications team are skilled professionals who live and breathe lean project management to bring *Cybersecurity Training* to life; thank you, Charlene Kronstedt. The Exeter team was fantastic in editing our book to their high standards! Thank you, Dhinesh and your team. Beth O'Malley, from Bond University, expertly converted the book cover into the correct file formats and sizes I struggled with; your technical expertise saved the day.

I thank my amazing family, mother, and my father, who was an educator! Finally, I would like to thank my coauthor, Chris Walker, who is a fantastic person, as confirmed by all those who know and love him.

Chris is a true leader and supported a large team to deliver successful training in a highly complex (VUCA) environment. A true servant leader: I learned so much from you, Chris. Thanks!

Uh-oh, Greg! If I have to thank everyone to whom I am grateful, I will put everyone to sleep and use way too many pages. Honestly, I have benefitted from so many opportunities, and I feel fortunate to have had a career that was so developmentally focused. Thank you to my dear friend Kaveh Bassiri, PhD, who taught me how to use Windows; to Kenneth Page, the late Dr. Steven Bornstein, Daniel Shimabuku, PhD, and Jeffrey Rapport, who believed in me and helped me in my early years at Kaiser Permanente; to Donna Young, Thea Giboney, Ellen Woo, Dr. Anina Schwartz, Dr. Peter Mathews, who gave me my initial role of leading large-scale training for KP HealthConnect. To my entire team and my dear KP HealthConnect colleagues—you know who you are, and you are my family! Among them are stars in instructional design, Joanne Howell, Michelle Mancha, Sandra Gehrer, Molly Uzoh, PhD, and Suzanne Viger. To Bill Craddock, Chit Mayor, Lina Shadid, Ramsi Bedeir, and Andrew Beer for transitioning me into IBM. To my team who followed me across the world and supported our success at CCAD: Arthur Chiu, Marc Chiu, Zainab Hafiz, Cletia Hart, Derek Molnar, Jessica Nguyen, and Crystal Priebe. To the many CCAD colleagues who made learning successful: Greg Skulmoski, PhD, Dr. Manish Kohli, Susan Ward, Michelle Machon, DNP, MSN, RN, CPHIMS, CENP, and many others.

One person has little idea about her impact on this book. In 2005, shortly after being chosen to lead Kaiser Permanente Northern California Region's Epic Ambulatory training effort, I attended the Epic User Group Meeting in Madison, Wisconsin. The most memorable and impactful presentation I saw there was delivered by Karis Meskimen, titled "Show Me Your ID," and was my first introduction to ADDIE and the Kirkpatrick Model. By that time, I had already been involved in training desktop software for more than eight years and in teaching adults for more than two decades, yet at that point, I had no idea about these formal instructional design frameworks. Thank you, Karis!

Finally, thanks to my sons Zakaria and Norm, to my daughter Angel, and my wife Silvia for putting up with my extreme work habits.

PART I

Cybersecurity Learning Ecosystem

"Businesses also operate in a world in which 95% of cybersecurity issues can be traced to human error" (World Economic Forum 2022, 52).

Introduction

Human error is the root cause of many cybersecurity incidents, and training can prevent and mitigate cybersecurity incidents. We interpret the alarming and widely reported World Economic Forum statistic of 95 percent to represent human errors made along the *entire* digital product or service life cycle, including poor engineering decisions leading to less secure digital products and services. While there is a lack of consensus on whether the number of cybersecurity incidents due to human error is as high as 95 percent, we avoid the "percentage debate." Instead, we focus on the solution in this book: cybersecurity awareness and training can provide skills and knowledge to prevent and mitigate the growing number and sophistication of cybersecurity threats. Microsoft researchers (2022, 109) conclude basic security hygiene protects against 98 percent of cybersecurity attacks. Indeed, as detailed in this book, we believe training can help develop a culture that values safe cybersecurity practices.

What is cybersecurity, and why do organizations and society require regular cybersecurity training? Cybersecurity is defending digital assets from attacks. Cybersecurity is risk management: identifying, protecting, detecting, responding, and recovering from malicious cyber events. Organizations require increased cybersecurity because there are more digital transformation projects; these digital products and services

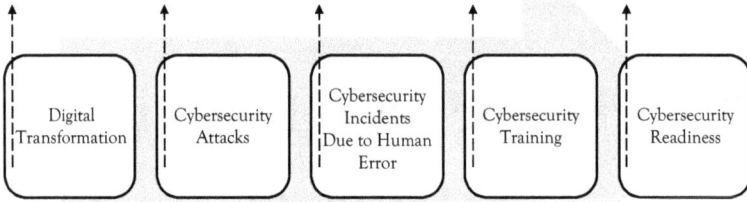

Figure I.1 Cybersecurity training and readiness

require cybersecurity. Unfortunately, not all these projects have fully addressed cybersecurity, resulting in expanded vulnerabilities and deficient cybersecurity readiness. A growing attack surface has invited more cyberattacks, drawing more government regulation and tightening insurance requirements.

Organizations can improve cybersecurity readiness by combining and tailoring best practices in standards, frameworks, and models like those from the International Organization for Standardization (ISO). Recall that human error is a significant cause of cybersecurity incidents. Many cybersecurity incidents can be prevented and mitigated with cybersecurity training. Never has cybersecurity training been prioritized and valued as we see it today and will be for years to come. Future digital transformation projects will be initiated to protect artificial intelligence (AI)-enabled systems, propelled by quantum technologies. More technologies. More cyberattacks. More cybersecurity. More cybersecurity training leads to improved cybersecurity readiness (Figure I.1).

Since the threat actors use more diverse and sophisticated techniques, cybersecurity training will be regularly offered and updated to maintain and optimize readiness.

Demand for Cybersecurity Training

One needs only to look at news headlines to see an increased focus on cybersecurity, cyberattacks, and opinion pieces. Since you are reading *Cybersecurity Training*, you are well aware of the threats and opportunities.

Indeed, you may be a participant, subject matter expert, or coordinator in your organization's Cybersecurity Awareness Month activities. What is driving the demand for more cybersecurity training?

Drivers: More Digital Transformation Projects

An online "digital transformation" search returns hundreds of millions of results. Organizations do not buy digital transformation from their favorite online store; they initiate project teams to plan, design, build, test, implement, and optimize systems. More digital transformation has resulted in more connected systems, data, and people. More people use more systems and from various locations with numerous devices. Organizational attack surfaces are expanding with each new digital transformation project. More digital transformation results in threat actors searching for cybersecurity vulnerabilities, leading to attacks on organizations and their people. Cybersecurity training can better prepare people to prevent and mitigate cybersecurity attacks.

Drivers: Increased Cyberattacks

The enlarged attack surface resulting from digital transformation projects has created more hacker opportunities. More opportunities have attracted more hackers. Why is there an increased number of cyberattacks? The return on investment to the hacker is relatively high; with a few clicks of the mouse and online payment, the novice hacker can access sophisticated hacking tools and services that improve their probability of success. One only needs to scan the headlines for ransomware payout to see that hackers can earn millions in their favorite currency. Therefore, with an ever-growing attack surface, organizations will continue to see growing cyberattacks with sophisticated cybersecurity capabilities.

Since the human element is a weak link in the cybersecurity ecosystem, we expect the demand for cybersecurity training to continue and increase. Indeed, CISA (Cybersecurity and Infrastructure Security Agency) contends that "More than 90% of successful cyberattacks start with a phishing email" (Cybersecurity and Infrastructure Security

Agency 2022). When hackers use new technologies and strategies, they target knowledge deficits that increase the likelihood of success. Cybersecurity knowledge deficits can be reduced through cybersecurity training (e.g., training helps learners identify potential phishing attacks and what to do about them).

Drivers: More Regulations and Insurance Compliance

We are not the only stakeholders that have observed the increase in successful cybersecurity attacks; governments and insurance providers have noticed and acted. Governments across the globe are drafting new regulations and strategies to address cybersecurity threats. Government reach and powers are expanding, especially in critical infrastructure industries (e.g., health care, defense, and finance) and critical technologies (e.g., biotechnology, cybersecurity, quantum, and robotics). Each country is different, resulting in different government approaches and degrees of regulatory reach and range. Nonetheless, the result will be more cybersecurity reporting and compliance requirements like auditing.

Insurance companies are raising cybersecurity insurance premiums due to large claims and damages. However, insurance premiums can be reduced with evidence of cybersecurity capabilities. Therefore, since the human element is a critical success factor in cybersecurity, organizations can expect more training activity to satisfy government regulators and insurers. However, regulators encourage compliance not because of the necessity of compliance, rather, they[2] hope organizations will align with best practices outlined in regulations, frameworks, and standards because adopting sound cybersecurity practices is good for organizations and good for those they serve.

---

[2] Greg Skulmoski participated and contributed to the new version of the NIST Cybersecurity Framework v2.0 and attended the *Journey to the NIST Cybersecurity Framework (CSF) 2.0 Workshop #2 and #3*, where a NIST organizer encouraged organizations to use the Framework because it represents best practices rather than adopt the NIST CSF 2.0 as a "tick-the-box" compliance exercise.

Drivers: Technological Arms Race

There is a technological arms race where organizations are upgrading systems, including cybersecurity software with AI capabilities, to improve their defense posture. Threat actors also invest in AI research and development to improve their attack capabilities. Organizations are responding by increasing their cybersecurity capabilities (e.g., identify, respond, and recover) delivered through projects. Thus, organizations and threat actors are in a continual improvement cycle: a cybersecurity arms race! New threats and technologies are driving additional cybersecurity training. The World Economic Forum (2022) advises organizations to prepare for a cybersecurity *disaster* due to quantum computing hacking capabilities. The attack surface is growing, creating more opportunities for threat actors and defensive cybersecurity projects and initiatives for many years to come. What can be done? We believe cybersecurity training and learning are critical success factors for cybersecurity readiness.

Cybersecurity Vulnerabilities Root Cause

When one investigates cyberattack root causes, one discovers that many cybersecurity incidents were due to human failure or had a human element to failure and prevention (IBM 2022, 32). We are less concerned about the precise percentage of cyberattacks due to human error since, from year to year, country to country, and industry to industry, the number of cybersecurity issues will fluctuate. Instead, we take a qualitative approach to gage the degree of cybersecurity incidents due to human error, such as very low, low, medium, high, and very high (more about Likert scale assessments later). Therefore, we assess the cybersecurity incidents due to human error is likely high for most organizations, and the precise number of incidents all organizations face varies with time.

What will likely remain constant for the foreseeable future is the necessity to address cybersecurity issues; organizations need to help their people (internal and external) manage the increasingly pervasive, confusing, and complex cybersecurity landscape. While the human element is an organization's greatest strength and its Achilles' Heel, cybersecurity training can prevent and mitigate many cybersecurity incidents. A fundamental principle in this book is that learning will be more successful if organizations build and optimize a learning ecosystem containing best practices outlined in training/education theory, frameworks, and models.

What Is Microlearning?

Traditional training involves attending a training course for a day or two. After a few months, learning retention decays unless it is refreshed or used. With microlearning, the learner continually acquires new knowledge that can be applied to real work. Microlearning can be more effective when the learner follows a learning to-do list or subscribes to online topics of interest. We offer microlearning opportunities to guide the leader to online resources to deepen their understanding of topics included in *Cybersecurity Training*.

Microlearning

Our microlearning sections provide a list of topics to further explore theories, standards, frameworks, models, processes, tools, templates, and other concepts for additional learning. We invite you to search[3] online or use regenerative AI technologies for more information about topics of interest. You may set up alerts to receive content covered in *Cybersecurity Training*:

- Find your industry's and discipline's digital transformation trends; training implications may exist.
- Search for cybersecurity trends in your industry and discipline; these may trigger training updates for your organization.
- Become familiar with privacy and cybersecurity-related regulations in your industry (NIST 2020a).
- What percentage of cybersecurity incidents is due to human error?

---

[3] We use the term "search and find online" to mean using online tools and resources to learn more about topics in the Microlearning sections. For example, we refer the reader to search for templates rather than direct them to a specific website because each reader has unique needs and interests.

State of the Art Training

We draw upon state-of-the-art training and education theory and our practical experiences to focus on learning to achieve a relatively permanent change in behavior or understanding. We define training as narrow development (e.g., cybersecurity awareness). In contrast, education may be defined as deeper, broader, and more sustained learning than training (e.g., a two-year Master of Cybersecurity education versus a one-month certification training course). To provide learning opportunities, we envision a learning ecosystem of people, technology, and processes with complex relationships focused on the learner. Within this evolving and adapting learning ecosystem, we provide a project management approach we have used to deliver training required for a cybersecurity-ready and resilient organization.

The learning ecosystem might have places where people can acquire foundational knowledge and learn from each other. There are practice areas to hone new skills and collaborate through cybersecurity playbook simulations. Ubiquitous learning is learning while you work; learning prompts can guide successful new task completion. With the advent of maturing metaverse technologies, we anticipate increasing digital opportunities like ubiquitous learning in the learning ecosystem.

Instructional Design

At the heart of a learning ecosystem is instructional design. Instructional design is the art and science of creating "detailed specifications" for developing, evaluating, and optimizing training (Hess and Greer 2016). Instructional design has a long history of international and interdisciplinary collaboration, resulting in a vast and diverse body of knowledge. Hess and Greer outline the principles of instructional design:

- *Process-based*: Instructional design is process-based, where steps are followed to achieve the desired learning outcomes. Process-based actions generally improve quality and are the foundation of technology management, cybersecurity, project management, risk management, and quality management.

- *Quality-focused*: Instructional design is focused on providing a learning experience that is consistent, reliable, and effective in achieving the training goals and objectives and learning outcomes.
- *Systems approach*: Instructional design aligns with systems theory, where the parts of the learning ecosystem are related and best understood holistically rather than in isolation.
- *Training goals*: A general statement about what the training program wishes to accomplish.
- *Training objectives*: Derived from the training goals and are specific statements about what the instructor intends to achieve.
- *Learning outcomes*: Describe the specific competencies the learner acquires due to the learning experience. Learning outcomes are measurable, indicating learning has occurred.

Later, the reader will see the ADDIE Model of Instructional Design includes these principles; indeed, project management, cybersecurity, and technology management are also process-based, quality-focused, with a systems approach to deliver value.

The Concept of Readiness

Organizations are on a quest for cybersecurity readiness, and we contend in this book that readiness can be improved and maintained through an organization's people (Figure I.1). With this goal, organizations can create and optimize their learning ecosystem. Training can improve cybersecurity competence, leading to improved readiness. Competence[4] is applying experience, skills, knowledge, attributes, and traits to achieve the desired outcome. What is readiness? The U.S. Department of Defense

---

[4] Greg's PhD dissertation *Project Participant Competence* examined competence along the project life cycle. A summary of the research was published by the Project Management Institute: G. Skulmoski and F. Hartman. March 2010. "Information Systems Project Manager Competencies: A Project Phase Investigation," *Project Management Journal*. 41, no. 1.

defines readiness as the ability to "fight and meet the demands of assigned missions." More specifically, readiness is the ability of organizations and people to predict and respond to cyber threats and opportunities. We include continual improvement practices for organizations to maintain and improve readiness. Your commitment to learning by reading this book indicates your commitment to continual improvement, a trait found in our most valued colleagues and leaders!

> *Cybersecurity readiness* is the ability to effectively apply and adapt the essential functions of cybersecurity (identify, protect, detect, respond, recover, and govern with continual improvement and adaptation cycles) to cyber threats and opportunities.

Effective organizations monitor, control, and report readiness-related KPIs (Key Performance Indicators) instead of thoughtless "tick-the-box" compliance to standards efforts. Cybersecurity readiness is multidimensional (people, processes, and technologies) and holistic. Cybersecurity readiness is not an endpoint; instead, it is continual in that organizations iteratively work to improve their posture. Improving cybersecurity readiness by improving the competence of people helps organizations leverage opportunities and prevent risks from becoming issues. Training is a fundamental method to improve competence and contribute to cybersecurity readiness.

Microlearning

The following topics can improve your understanding and application of learning-related topics related to organizational readiness:

- Search online for "ubiquitous learning" and how it is being used to improve work.
- Can you find articles about the metaverse that is emerging in your industry?
- Generate with AI the "big" learning and teaching trends in your industry.

The ADDIE Model of Instructional Design

How can organizations provide training so they are ready to address cybersecurity risks or leverage opportunities? When one reviews the literature about training, one quickly finds the ADDIE Model of Instructional Design: analyze, design, develop, implement, and evaluate training (Figure I.2). The ADDIE Model is an example of an instructional design process to develop training programs systematically. Instructional design emerged from post-World War II research by the U.S. military to create effective and manageable training programs. Researchers at Florida State University originally developed the ADDIE Model for the U.S. armed forces in the 1970s. Thus, the instructional design has a long history of research, practice, and improvement, reflected in the ADDIE Model. "There are more than 100 different variations of the [ADDIE] model; however, almost all of them reflect the generic 'ADDIE' process—analysis, design, develop, implement, and evaluate" (Allen 2006, 430). ADDIE may be applied as a linear or an iterative process.

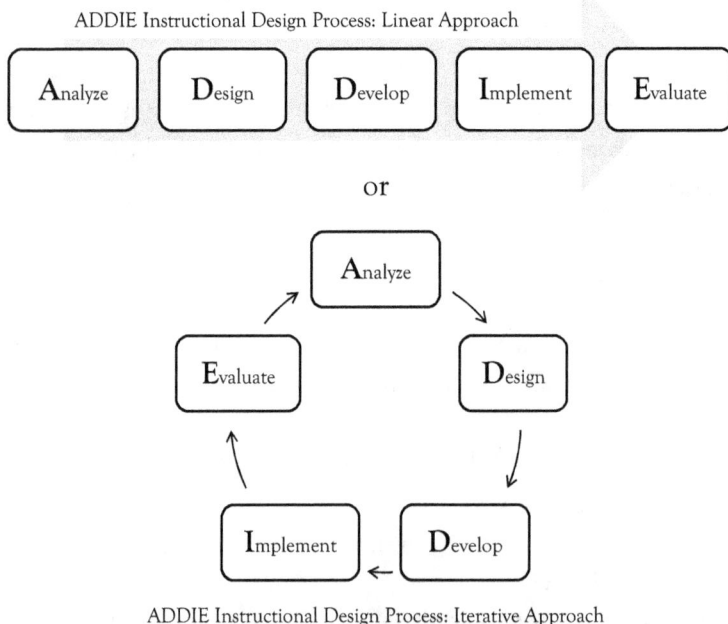

ADDIE Instructional Design Process: Linear Approach

| Analyze | Design | Develop | Implement | Evaluate |

or

ADDIE Instructional Design Process: Iterative Approach

Figure I.2 ADDIE Model of Instructional Design delivery approaches

Perhaps the pervasiveness and longevity of the ADDIE Model are due to researcher input from many disciplines (cognitive and behavioral psychology, systems engineering, instructional technology, and human performance improvement) to arrive at the robust, simple, and flexible ADDIE Model of Instructional Design. The ADDIE Model is suitable for training and education applications ranging from developing and delivering nontechnical to technical content like cybersecurity (Razali et al. 2019). Some experts conclude the ADDIE Model of Instructional Design is "most frequently used" by training practitioners to systematically create and evaluate learning experiences (Hess and Greer 2016, 267).

The original ADDIE approach was linear; however, others have represented the ADDIE Model in an iterative fashion (Peterson 2003, 228; Allen and Sites 2012, 38). Instructional design work is about the same whether the designer takes a linear (ADDIE Model project delivery method) or an iterative approach (ADDIE Model iterations for continual improvement). Later, we combine two ADDIE Model Instructional Design delivery approaches: First, we recommend[5] organizations implement the initial training with a linear project management approach. They may provide a minimum amount of training (also known as a "vanilla" or a minimum viable curriculum). Second, continue training as required and add new content by following an iterative instructional design approach with ADDIE iterations (Figure I.2). Notice that the work (the verbs) is the same whether a linear or iterative approach to instructional design is followed.

The sponsor[6] might be invited to review and approve outputs from each ADDIE phase so that stage gate governance improves the probability of training success. For example, the sponsor might review a one-page learning analysis document detailing competency gaps. A one-page design document may outline the training design. The entire developed suite of training artifacts (e.g., learner materials, facilitator

---

[5] Our recommendations and content in *Cybersecurity Training* are "applicable to most cybersecurity training projects, most of the time." This rubric was used by Greg Skulmoski when he was on the 2000 PMBOK® Guide Update Team.

[6] Project sponsors usually fund, manage, monitor, and control the overall project delivery but are less involved in the project manager's daily activities.

Table I.1 ADDIE model considerations

Analyze	1. What are the cybersecurity training goals? 2. What are the learners' characteristics? 3. What are the characteristics of the context or environment? 4. What resources are available? 5. How should the cybersecurity training be delivered?
Design	1. What are the cybersecurity learning outcomes? 2. What training methods will instructors use? 3. How should learners feel as they experience the training? 4. Do the learning outcomes align with the training objectives? 5. How will learning be assessed?
Develop	1. How will the training be provided (LMS? Face-to-Face? etc.) 2. What tools will be used to create the learning assets? 3. What training materials will be used (learner and facilitator)? 4. How will the pilot study be executed?
Implement	1. Are instructional methods working correctly? 2. Can discrepancies be addressed during training? 3. Are new cybersecurity training issues emerging?
Evaluate	1. To what degree were learning outcomes achieved? 2. What other forms of unstructured feedback are available? 3. How efficient were the training methods? 4. Were there any technical incidents? 5. Are there any new training opportunities? 6. Were there any outcomes that surprised us?

guide, assessment instruments, videos, simulations, leaderboards, LMS—learning management system—build, etc.) might be provided to the sponsor for review and approval. Workshops (ideally, face-to-face) rather than through e-mails are an expeditious way to review and approve. At each ADDIE phase (after Mayfield 2011, 21), the instructional designer can ask a series of questions (Table I.1).

Later, we expand and apply the ADDIE Model to cybersecurity training within the project delivery approach (Figure II.3).

Bloom's Taxonomy

Benjamin Bloom's Taxonomy is a hierarchical model of critical thought with six levels of increasing cognitive complexity (Figure I.3). Bloom's fundamental assumption is some types of learning need more cognitive processing than others. As the learner progresses through the Taxonomy

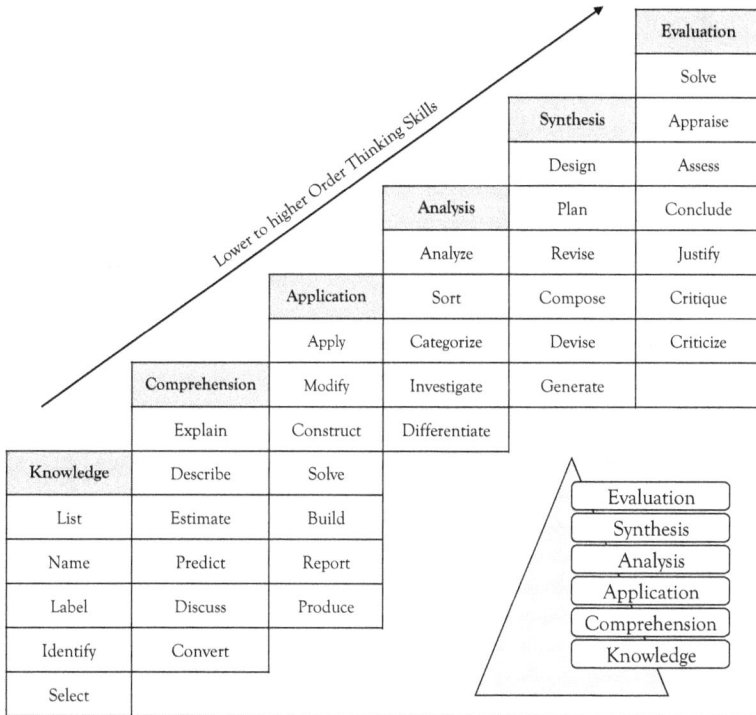

Figure I.3 Bloom's Taxonomy

levels, each cognitive level is subsumed by the next higher level (e.g., when learners work at the *application* level, they also draw upon learning from the *knowledge* and *comprehension* levels). Activity examples (e.g., modify, construct, and solve) at each level of cognitive thought are included in Figure I.3. Like the Kirkpatrick Model of Evaluation and the ADDIE Model of Instructional Design, Bloom's Taxonomy has matured and is widely applied. The models, frameworks, and standards in *Cybersecurity Training* recommend tailoring their tools, concepts, and processes to an organization's unique circumstances.

The levels of cognitive complexity in Bloom's Taxonomy (after Forehand 2010, 3) begin with less complex cognitive progressing to higher-order thinking:

1. *Knowledge*: retrieving relevant knowledge from long-term memory;
2. *Comprehension*: constructing meaning through interpreting;
3. *Application*: carrying out or using a procedure;

4. *Analysis*: breaking down material into smaller components to determine how they relate to one another and the overall structure;

5. *Synthesis*: putting together or rearranging elements to create something new; and

6. *Evaluation*: making judgments based on criteria and standards.

When instructional designers craft training, they align learning outcomes with the appropriate level of Bloom's Taxonomy to improve learning. For example, instructional designers avoid making a learning activity overly complex (e.g., synthesis level) for simple learning outcomes (e.g., comprehension level). Nor do they develop simple assessments when they design training for a technical role requiring advanced critical thought to complete highly technical cybersecurity tasks.

There are many benefits to using Bloom's Taxonomy in the instructional design process:

1. Facilitates planning and alignment between standards, training goals and objectives, and learning outcomes with training products, activities, and evaluation.

2. Reduces confusion and ambiguity with a generally accepted framework of classifying thinking.

3. Signals the level of complexity of activities as one progresses through the hierarchy.

4. Communicates expectations to the learner through a visual hierarchy.

5. Helps create appropriate assessments based on the desired level of cognitive complexity.

6. Provides a learning pathway to higher-order skills.

Therefore, when instructional designers craft training and evaluation, they are guided by training goals and objectives, and learning outcomes. They design with Bloom's Taxonomy in mind. While Bloom's Taxonomy has critics (e.g., learning is not always linear and discrete, and lower levels of cognitive thought can have equal value as higher levels, etc.), it is still widely used. In *Cybersecurity Training*, we leverage the Taxonomy's strengths to guide instructional design activities to provide appropriate learning experiences in corporate and university settings.

Kirkpatrick Model of Evaluation

"The Kirkpatrick Model continues to be useful, appropriate, and applicable in a variety of contexts. It is adaptable to many training environments and achieves high performance in evaluating training. The overview of publications on the Kirkpatrick Model shows that research using the model is an active and growing area" (Alsalamah and Callinan 2022, 36).

Organizations provide training not to demonstrate that training occurred. Instead, the training creates the conditions under which the desired learning may occur. Those conditions should include a psychologically safe environment in which learners can try out new skills without fear; modeling of target behaviors and skills by the instructor or the designed materials; treatment of error management (what not to do, how to troubleshoot, or seek help); and most importantly, practice opportunities. Practice opportunities should be provided in a setting and under conditions that mimic the learner's environment in real life. To determine whether the desired learning occurs, instructional designers and instructors evaluate learning (the "E" in ADDIE). We use and recommend the de facto standard: the Kirkpatrick Model of Evaluation (also known as Kirkpatrick's Four Levels of Training Evaluation).

The Kirkpatrick Model guides evaluation along the training impact chain, beginning with training, applying learning on the job, and transferring benefits to the organization. Learning refers to the knowledge, skills, and attitudes resulting from the training program (Kirkpatrick 1983, 19–20). A development process is added to the ADDIE Model to reflect those activities required to provide training (Figure I.4). Kirkpatrick's four levels of training evaluation include (1) the learner's reaction to the training, (2) learning evaluation, (3) the application of learning to one's job, and (4) the impact of training on the organization. Others have modified the Kirkpatrick Model by adding a higher evaluation level to evaluate the impact of training on society (Molenda and Pershing 2004) or to transform the linearity of the Kirkpatrick Model to an iterative approach to evaluation (Allen and Sites 2011) or to evaluate

Project Responsibility | Business Responsibility

Lessons Learned   *Assessment*

| Development Process | Reaction and Learning | Application | Organizational Impact |

Low ←————— *Complexity of Assessment* —————→ High

In Scope
For the training team

Out of Scope
For the training team

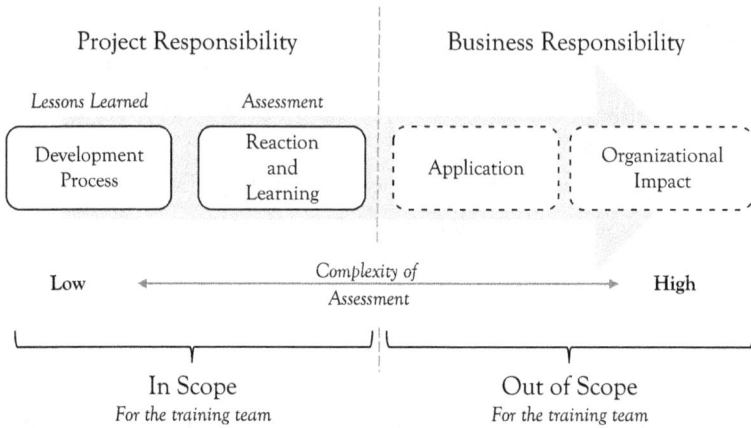

Figure I.4 Training chain of impact and the Kirkpatrick Model of Evaluation

the training return on investment (Bailey n.d.). While the Kirkpatrick Model of Evaluation is decades old, it is commonly used in practice by businesses and research (Alsalamah and Callinan 2022).

The Kirkpatrick Model of Evaluation goes beyond traditional evaluation (reaction and learning) to evaluate the degree to which the training has been applied to one's job and whether the training has impacted the organization (Figure I.4). Others have modified the Kirkpatrick Model to address "weaknesses" and included a pretraining evaluation of the project's development phase. We align project management activities with the generally accepted ADDIE Model: analyze training requirements, design, develop, implement, and evaluate training (Figure II.3).

The Kirkpatrick Model is applicable in the project context because it guides evaluation responsibilities for the project team (development process, reaction, and learning) and the business owner (application and organizational impact). The training sponsor (also known as the product or service owner) represents the business interests. The line between the project and business world is permeable in that organizations can do things on the project side to improve the probability of successful transfer of learning (see planning and design phases).

We recommend and often assess learning with multiple-choice questions to determine whether learning outcomes have been achieved.

We conduct a lessons learned evaluation about the ADDIE Method that created the training and supporting artifacts such as the facilitator guide. We ask questions about the learner's opinion of the training, environment, the trainer, food served at lunch, training handouts, and so on. While some may question the usefulness of reaction assessments, assessing a learner's reaction to training is justified as part of continual improvement. Since organizations are spending resources to train, they assess the effectiveness and efficiency of training; sometimes, learner reaction feedback can lead to significant improvements. For example, a learner may provide constructive feedback about changing how learning resources are presented, resulting in improved usability. The reader will see later that the Kirkpatrick Model of Evaluation provides a straightforward framework to determine whether learning has occurred (we prefer simple rather than complex approaches for most project activities—an Occam's razor[7] mindset).

A critical link in Kirkpatrick's Model of Evaluation chain of impact is the challenging task of assessing the degree learning has been applied to one's job: "The measurement of behavior refers to the on-the-job changes in behavior that occur because of attendance at the training program" (Kirkpatrick 1983). While there are actions the project team can take to improve learning transfer, assessing the degree to which the learner applies the new competencies to one's job falls on the business side of the training equation. The learner's manager is better positioned to assess learning that might not be demonstrated until three or more months after training. However, the instructional designer will seek feedback from the learner's manager or others about how well the learnings were applied (Figure II.22). Therefore, assessing Kirkpatrick's application of learning is out of scope for the project team.

---

[7] Occam's razor (also known as the law of parsimony) is a philosophical approach where one selects the simplest explanation to get to the truth or to understand something. Occam was an English Franciscan friar in the 14th century. With apologies to real philosophers, we extend the spirit of Occam's razor to our lean approaches in training and project management.

Kirkpatrick (1983) outlined the necessary conditions for learning to be successfully transferred to the job (Application, Figure I.4):

- Learners must have the desire to change.
- Learners have the necessary knowledge and skills to try the new behavior.
- Management allows or encourages change.
- Management is willing to help.
- Learners are rewarded for successfully applying new competencies.

The final link (or level) in Kirkpatrick's chain of impact is to assess whether and to what degree the training has impacted the organization (Figure I.4): "The most significant factors but the most difficult to measure are the training program results. Was productivity increased? Quality improved? Costs reduced?" (Kirkpatrick 1983, 24). While it is theoretically attractive to strive to assess the impact of training on the organization, it is also highly complex for many reasons: there are intervening factors, like learner motivation, managerial support, self-efficacy, goal setting, and others, that affect learner performance and organizational impact.

Indeed, sometimes applying what has been learned may be delayed because the competency-triggering event does not occur (e.g., discovering someone in distress and the need to apply CPR [cardiopulmonary resuscitation] training that was taken three years ago). However, applying new competencies can be encouraged through gamification techniques like pointsification,[8] leaderboards, and rewards. Therefore, measuring the impact of training on organizational performance is not only out of scope but also complex and likened to searching for the Holy Grail (Tamkin et al. 2002, 45): "It is universally agreed that evaluation at the behavioral and results levels are made more difficult since training is not the only

---

[8] Pointsification: providing points for successful learning or engagement that are tallied on a leaderboard. Earning points for correct answers often engages learners resulting in improved learning.

relevant causal factor" (Tamkin et al. 2002, 42). Despite the generally accepted position that evaluating the impact of learning on the organization is problematic, increasingly, training departments are pressured to justify training investments.

This final chain of impact link in Kirkpatrick's Model has also been criticized for not going far enough; some critics propose evaluating the degree to which the training has impacted the broader society (Molenda and Pershing 2004). If measuring training's impact on the organization was not challenging enough, measuring the impact of training on society would be complex and resource-intensive. Therefore, these operational considerations (evaluating learner performance and training impact on the organization and society) are best left to others. In *Cybersecurity Training*, we focus on the project side of training and evaluate the reaction to training and the initial attainment of learning (Figure I.4). We will also evaluate the training development activities as part of the lessons learned.

In resource-constrained organizations, higher-value activities like practicing using response and recovery playbooks with a CSIRT (computer security incident response team) may be a better use of resources than evaluating at the higher levels of Kirkpatrick's training evaluations in a dynamic environment. Cybersecurity awareness and specialized role-based training are no longer desirable; they have become an operational necessity.

Microlearning

Find online more resources about evaluation:

- Is the Kirkpatrick Model of Evaluation still relevant?
- Use regenerative AI to write an outline to evaluate training.

Learning Ecosystem Technologies

Learning management systems (LMS) are the most common way to manage training and learning. LMS evolve like other technologies in pursuing innovation. We expect organizations to regularly patch and upgrade LMS, resulting in functionality and workflow improvements. Therefore, organizations will leverage innovative LMS capabilities to improve their ADDIE-based corporate training programs like cybersecurity general awareness training. In PART II, we address LMS more directly when we plan, design, configure, test, and implement LMS classrooms and functionality to support training.

Technical Frameworks and Standards Alignment

Each industry has technical frameworks and standards that guide organizations to provide their goods and services according to best practices. Standards like those from ISO (International Organization for Standardization) outline best practices for quality (e.g., ISO 9001), safety requirements for industrial robots (ISO 10218), and many others. While standards are usually rigid and accepted globally as best practices, they allow for tailoring to fit the organization's needs. Frameworks also represent best practices but usually exist without well-defined and globally accepted standards. Frameworks are less prescriptive and more flexible than standards. However, robust and widely accepted frameworks (e.g., NIST Cybersecurity Framework) may coexist with standards (e.g., ISO/IEC 27000:2018 Information security management systems).

The value proposition is if you judiciously apply the standard or framework, you are more likely to achieve the right quality while minimizing risks. Therefore, to provide cybersecurity training to achieve readiness, we align best practices in global standards and frameworks in this book (Table I.2).

While we have chosen to use the PMBOK® Guide for project management, we could have used another framework like PRINCE2. Or we may have used ISO/IEC 27000:2018 Information security management systems rather than the NIST Cybersecurity Framework. The frameworks and standards we use in *Cybersecurity Training* represent best practices and are generally accepted and applicable to most projects in most industries and disciplines most of the time. The PMBOK® Guide is used as the

Table I.2 Standards and frameworks in cybersecurity training

Name	Best practice
A Guide to the Project Management Body of Knowledge (PMBOK® Guide)	Standard
ISO 9001 Quality Management	Standard
ISO 31000 Risk Management	Standard
NIST (National Institute of Standards and Technology) Cybersecurity Framework	Framework
ITIL (Information Technology Infrastructure Library) for Technology Management	Framework
ADDIE (Analyze Design Develop Implement Evaluate) Instructional Design	Framework
Kirkpatrick Model of Evaluation	Framework
Bloom's Taxonomy of Cognitive Thinking	Framework

authors have extensive experience with this standard[9]; however, PRINCE2 project management practitioners can apply the concepts in *Cybersecurity Training* to their cybersecurity projects. In past projects, we followed the NIST Cybersecurity Framework and ISO/IEC 27000:2018 Information security management systems standard. We use the NIST Cybersecurity Framework in *Cybersecurity Training* because it is theoretically and practically sound, freely available in multiple languages, and has the robust support of the American government. There are few viable alternatives to the ADDIE Model of Instructional Design, Bloom's Taxonomy, and the Kirkpatrick Model of Evaluation for training purposes; therefore, we align to these global de facto frameworks in this book.

Ultimately, no single framework will comprehensively match every operational context. The best frameworks permit themselves to be tailored to the context. We encourage practitioners to rely on their experience

---

[9] Greg Skulmoski was on the Project Management Institute's *PMBOK® Guide Update Committee* that reviewed and updated the first edition of the PMBOK® Guide (1996) and released the second edition in 2000 to coincide with the new millennium. Greg acted in the role of project management SME and author on the *Update Project Team* (see PMBOK® Guide 2000 Edition, Appendix C.2).

and discernment in adopting, tailoring, and combining the most relevant components to their project and organization.

Information Technology Infrastructure Library

Organizations use e-mails, finance, human resources, manufacturing, productivity (e.g., spreadsheets) applications, and other digital services IT departments provide. IT departments regularly manage a catalog of hundreds of digital services for which end users are grateful. The IT department plans, implements, manages, and optimizes these digital services, which may follow the Information Technology Infrastructure Library (ITIL). While other digital services frameworks (e.g., COBIT and ISO IEC 20000) exist, ITIL might be the most popular and widely adopted.[10]

ITIL Overview

What is ITIL? It is a framework of best practices to deliver and manage an expanding suite of digital products and services. ITIL provides a comprehensive, holistic, and systematic approach to delivering value, managing risks and quality, implementing lean practices, and providing a predictable and stable technical ecosystem that supports organizational growth and innovation. The ITIL way of delivering and managing technology is one of the most globally popular frameworks and, therefore, can be considered the global de facto standard (Tsunoda and Kino 2018, 1). ITIL's popularity is due to its benefits, like increased productivity and digital performance, improved value realization and customer satisfaction, reduced costs, better return on digital investments, and enhanced communication through common concepts, processes, and terminology.

ITIL Service Value System

Organizations begin their ITIL journey by following the ITIL Service Value System (Figure I.5). The Service Value System outlines how to create and deliver products and services to consumers (AXELOS Limited

---

[10] ITL is more fully explained and integrated with project management in *Shields Up: Cybersecurity Project Management*. However, the principles in *Shields Up* and *Cybersecurity Training* apply to projects and cybersecurity training in a COBIT technology environment.

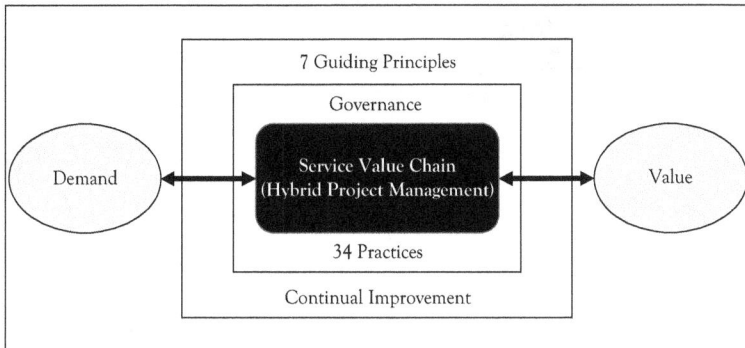

Figure I.5 ITIL Service Value System

2019, 66). The Service Value Chain process begins when a demand triggers a request for a new product or service (e.g., improve cybersecurity detection capabilities or update cybersecurity training).

A project (the Service Value Chain in ITIL terminology) is initiated, planned, designed, built, tested, and handed over to IT operations for implementation. IT operations manages the digital service to provide value to the end users. The IT team continually improves the digital products and services they manage (Figure I.5).

ITIL includes 34 "practices" (e.g., Strategy Management practice) that guide the IT team to provide digital products and services. Similarly, 10 "knowledge areas" in the sixth edition of the PMBOK® Guide embody project management best practices (e.g., Project Risk Management). There is alignment between the best practices in the PMBOK® Guide and the ITIL framework (e.g., risk and quality management are prominent in both), which makes the project team valued partners with the IT operational teams.

The ITIL Strategy Management practice guides the organization to develop and implement an IT services strategy valued by their customers (Figure I.6). When a new service is requested (e.g., improve cybersecurity detection capabilities), the IT team follows the Service Request Management practice to initiate a new project (ITIL's Service Value Chain, Figure I.5). The team also follows the Project Management practice to implement the new digital product (e.g., robotics) or service (e.g., cybersecurity software) within the ITIL framework. The tools and processes described in the ITIL Project Management practice align with common project management standards like the PMBOK® Guide and the ADDIE Model of Instructional Design.

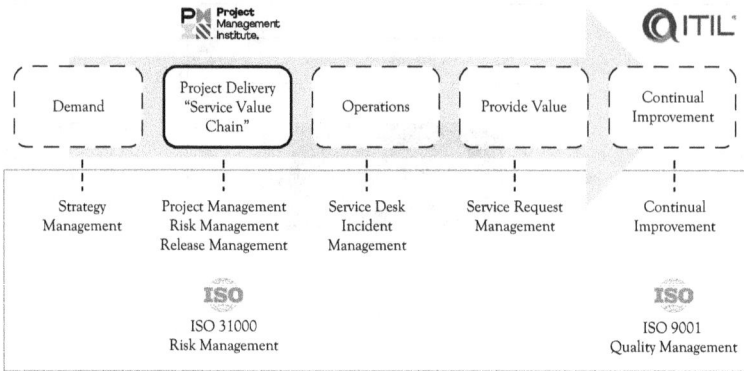

Figure I.6 ITIL practices and Service Value System

The project manager collaborates with the release manager, who follows the ITIL Release Management practice to bring the new digital product or service safely and securely to the end users. (We recommend project managers invite the release manager to the project planning workshop to plan the tail end of projects.) When a new digital service or product is used, and an error occurs, the end user can contact the service desk for help, which provides an incident tracking number. Organizations may follow the Service Desk and Incident Management practices to resolve digital problems. ITIL's Continual Improvement practice also guides the IT department. ITIL practices align with the project management standard outlined in the PMBOK® Guide and ISO risk and quality management. The *Golden Promise* that brings all these frameworks and standards together is if you tailor and apply the standard or framework, you are more likely to deliver the right quality while preventing risks.

Like other standards and frameworks, ITIL includes principles to guide decisions and actions when completing work in the Service Value Chain. Principles direct how people act in *all* situations. Adopting these principles increases the likelihood of a common approach to delivering services and products. These principles apply to Service Value Chain activities (AXELOS Limited 2019, 47–48) including training:

1. *Focus on value*: Ensure all activities create value, directly or indirectly, for the organization, users, and/or other stakeholders. Value is subjective and includes the digital product or service's perceived benefits, utility, and significance (e.g., cybersecurity training).

2. *Start where you are*: Apply lean thinking to value chain activities, optimizing existing products and services (e.g., training materials) before discarding what exists and initiating a new project. ITIL practitioners leverage what is available to reduce waste through a systematic measuring, observing, and improving process (the Lean Six Sigma method aligns neatly with this principle).

3. *Progress iteratively with feedback*: Deliver services incrementally (Figure I.2), if possible, rather than all at once to reduce risk and improve the probability of delivering the intended value. Therefore, look for opportunities to break up projects into multiple, smaller projects (e.g., phases 1 and 2). Build-in regular feedback opportunities to ensure value is delivered (Figure II.22). An iterative approach aligns with adaptive delivery approaches like agile scrums (Figure I.17).

4. *Collaborate and promote visibility*: Provide services (e.g., cybersecurity training) through the Service Value Chain, often in teams where collaboration can lead to improved engagement, support, commitment, lasting outcomes, understanding, trust, and cooperation. Sharing visibility also contributes to these positive outcomes.

5. *Think and work holistically*: Understand value from a holistic or system perspective rather than a collection of individual components. Value is increased when the Service Value System (Figure I.5), four dimensions of service management, and these principles are coordinated and integrated. Visibility into the entire service value stream improves understanding, management, and control. The think-and-work holistically principle is good cybersecurity practice.

6. *Keep it simple and practical*: Endeavor to complete Service Value Chain activities with a minimum number of steps. Lean thinking and other adaptive techniques are encouraged (e.g., "Goldilocks Principle[11]")

7. *Optimize and automate*: Look for opportunities to improve the Service Value Chain to maximize the value of our services and products. Increasingly, people use technology and automation with continual

---

[11] A 19th-century fairy tale where Goldilocks, the main character, who did not want too much, nor too little; Goldilocks always wanted just the right amount. However, the moral of the story is not to enter someone's home without their permission; appropriate advice for hackers.

improvement methods like Lean Six Sigma to guide process improvements (Figure I.19). A recurring theme in this book is to design in continual improvement processes embedded in the frameworks and standards.

These principles should guide the organization in all circumstances, even if there are changes to organizational goals, personnel, project type, and so on. The ITIL principles are intended to shape organizational culture in all activities (e.g., projects and operations) along the Service Value System (AXELOS Limited 2019). The organization's culture comprises beliefs, values, assumptions, and principles guiding our interactions. Training can help shape the organization's culture, especially when its leadership consistently models the desired organizational culture.

These ITIL principles relate to "service management," which can be broadly applied. For example, re-read these ITIL technology principles and see how many apply to your discipline. For example, most of these principles can be applied to manufacturing, research and development, disaster relief, and training. If you review the ADDIE Model of Instructional Design, you can relate these ITIL principles to cybersecurity training. The ITIL framework includes a governance function (policies, procedures, rules, tools, methods, etc.) to align IT services with organizational strategy and goals. Therefore, when we deliver technology and training projects, we combine and tailor best practices and principles from a broad range of standards and frameworks as detailed in *Cybersecurity Training*.

Thus, ITIL 4 has a holistic framework for managing technology services such as cybersecurity projects. ITIL 4 supports tailoring the framework to the organization, context, and project; hybrid project delivery is supported: "the ITIL SVS [Service Value System] supports many approaches such as agile, DevOps and Lean, as well as traditional process and project management, with a flexible value-oriented operating model" (AXELOS Limited 2019, 44). ITIL 4 provides a comprehensive service management framework that supports cybersecurity efforts, including training.

Microlearning

Technology management is a growing discipline and research area; indeed, most universities provide degrees related to technology management, in addition to professional certifications like ITIL Foundation. Go online to discover more about managing digital technologies:

- What is the difference between COBIT and ITIL?
- What is the COBIT maturity model?

NIST Cybersecurity Framework

Most cybersecurity frameworks are based on risk and quality management; therefore, cybersecurity frameworks share common elements like principles, processes, competencies, technologies, and governance aimed at delivering products and services at the appropriate level of quality while minimizing risks. In *Cybersecurity Training,* we use the NIST Cybersecurity Framework as it applies to any industry or sector of any size, whether domestic or international. The U.S. Department of Commerce makes the NIST Cybersecurity Framework freely available in multiple languages with regularly updated documents. Therefore, we use the NIST Cybersecurity Framework in *Cybersecurity Training* since it applies to most cybersecurity projects. There are other general cybersecurity standards like the ISO/IEC 27000:2018 Information technology—Security techniques—Information security management systems—Overview and vocabulary (often shortened to ISO/IEC 27001:2022 Information security management systems standard or ISO/IEC 27000), ISO 28000 Security and resilience—Security management systems—Requirements, or industry-specific cybersecurity standards like the Australian Prudential Standard CPS 234 for deposit receiving institutions. However, whether the framework is NIST or something else, the fundamental principles, processes, and tools outlined in *Cybersecurity Training* can guide cybersecurity training. The NIST Cybersecurity Framework Core outlines its cybersecurity approach.

NIST Framework Core

The NIST Framework Core includes six cybersecurity functions (objectives) and related categories (desired outcomes). Each category is further divided into subcategories. The value proposition is organizations can tailor their cybersecurity strategy and operations based on these six functions and systematically improve their cybersecurity readiness. Thus, the NIST Framework Core guides organizations (Table I.3) with cybersecurity functions (6), categories (22), and subcategories (106). We detail the *Awareness and Training* (AT) subcategory in the *Protect* (PR) category in PART II of *Cybersecurity Training*.

The increase in cybersecurity budgets results in a continuous flow of projects to improve these NIST functions and categories as new technologies (AI and later quantum) are introduced into digital ecosystems.

NIST Implementation Tiers

The NIST Cybersecurity Framework includes four implementation tiers that offer cybersecurity improvement and target state guidance

Table I.3 NIST functions (6) and categories (22)

Govern	Identify	Protect	Detect	Respond	Recover
Organizational Context	Asset Management	**Awareness and Training**	Continuous Monitoring	Incident Management	Incident Recovery Plan Execution
Risk Management Strategy	Risk Assessment	Identity Management and Access Control	Adverse Event Analysis	Incident Analysis	Incident Recovery Communication
Cybersecurity Supply Chain Management	Improvement	Data Security	–	Incident Response Reporting and Communication	–
Roles, Responsibilities, and Authorities	–	Platform Security	–	Incident Mitigation	–
Policies, Processes, and Procedures	–	Technology Infrastructure Resilience	–	–	–
Oversight	–	–	–	–	–

(Figure I.7, after NIST 2023, 12–14). Fundamentally, one progresses through the tiers when cybersecurity risk management improves, becomes more integrated, and has external stakeholder participation. Since people are a significant pillar of the information technology ecosystem (people, process, and technology), one can only move through the tiers if an organization's people (internal and external) have sufficient cybersecurity awareness and training leading to readiness.

Often, more cybersecurity training (e.g., specialized) is required to progress through the tiers and remain ready. Readers may review the Cybersecurity Capability Maturity Model (C2M2) for additional insight into maturity pathways, including training (Office of Cybersecurity, Energy Security, and Emergency Response 2022, 61).

NIST Framework Profiles

The organization can analyze its current business objectives, threat environment, and requirements/controls and use the NIST Cybersecurity Framework to arrive at its framework profile, also known as its *current state* (Figure I.8). The NIST Cybersecurity Framework can help the organization identify and plan for an improved future *target state*. The target profile includes the desired outcomes (e.g., something of value) to achieve the organization's cybersecurity risk management goals. Indeed, an organization can have multiple profiles addressing different cybersecurity risks with different probabilities of occurrence and impact levels (e.g., the detect function may be weaker than the current state's response function). The organization's awareness and training capabilities are reflected in the current state, and improvements through awareness, training, and learning will appear in the target state.

Given the complexity of cybersecurity, the NIST Cybersecurity Framework is not a standalone framework; there are over 1,300 NIST reference materials, including the NICE Workforce Framework, NIST controls, awareness, and specialized role-based training (Figure I.9). Therefore, NIST document(s) may be combined and tailored to meet the unique requirements of organizations, including cybersecurity training. A NIST cybersecurity audit might identify gaps that can be

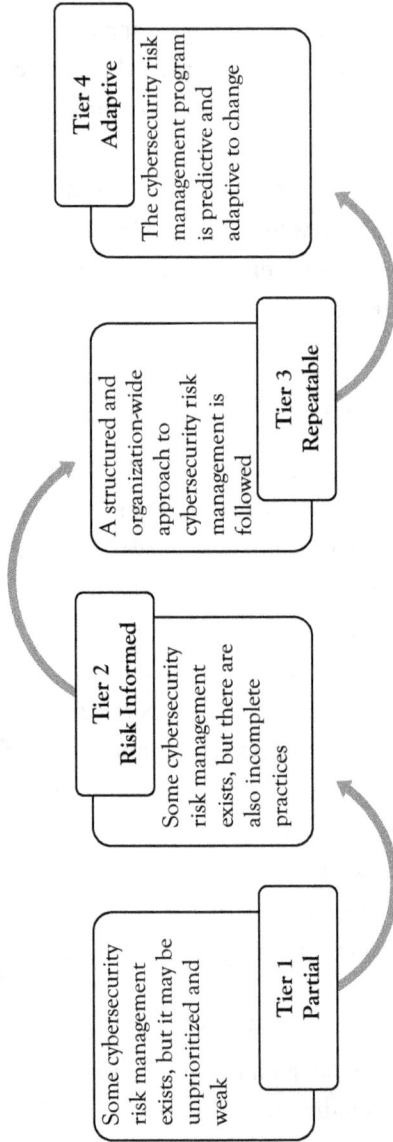

Tier 4 Adaptive
The cybersecurity risk management program is predictive and adaptive to change

Tier 3 Repeatable
A structured and organization-wide approach to cybersecurity risk management is followed

Tier 2 Risk Informed
Some cybersecurity risk management exists, but there are also incomplete practices

Tier 1 Partial
Some cybersecurity risk management exists, but it may be unprioritized and weak

Figure I.7 NIST implementation tiers

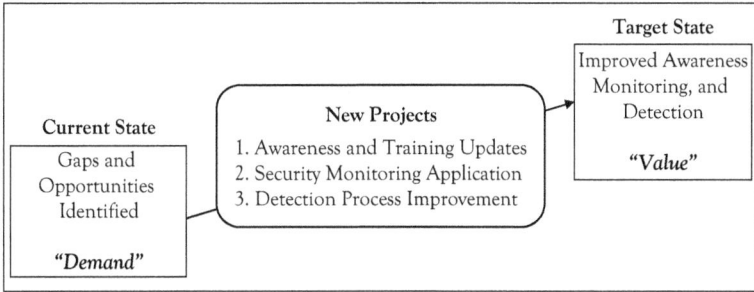

Figure I.8 NIST profiles—current and target state example

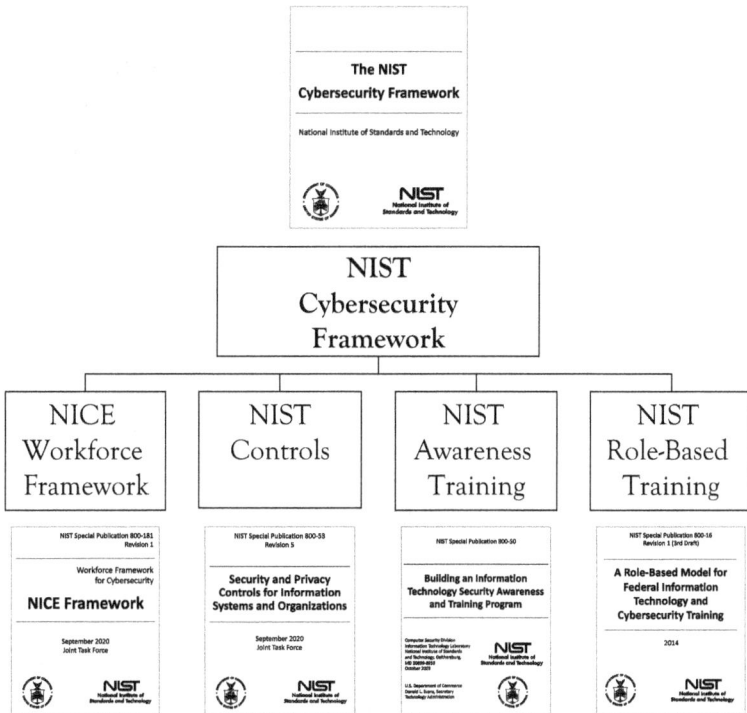

Figure I.9 NIST Cybersecurity Framework—cybersecurity training

addressed through improved cybersecurity training resulting in NIST tier progression. The ISO 19001 Guidelines for Auditing Management Systems can provide similar guidance for cybersecurity systems auditing.

Most cybersecurity standards and frameworks include components like the NIST Cybersecurity Framework, such as an overarching framework, controls, requirements, and perhaps a competency model. The NIST Cybersecurity Framework is favored for its comprehensive family of supporting materials that are regularly updated and widely accessible, and we have aligned with the NIST Cybersecurity Framework in our practice.

NICE Workforce Framework

The NICE (National Initiative for Cybersecurity Education) Workforce Framework for Cybersecurity (Figure I.9) is a competency model that details skills and knowledge to complete cybersecurity tasks (NIST 2020b). These building blocks can be used to improve the organization's workforce capacity to manage cybersecurity risks. People can improve their cybersecurity capabilities when they improve their competence, defined as a collection of skills and knowledge (Figure I.10A). To complete a cybersecurity task, one uses a combination of skills and knowledge (Figure I.10B). A cybersecurity position requires competencies to complete its tasks (Figure I.10C). The organization can categorize the IT department's many roles into a smaller subset of tasks for training purposes (Figure I.10D). Finally, the NICE Workforce Framework may be followed to develop an internal cybersecurity credential like a digital badge based on acquiring new competencies (Figure I.10E).

By breaking down work into task statements (skills and knowledge), NICE Workforce Framework users have a common understanding of cybersecurity work. The NICE Workforce Framework can help organizations develop training to meet cybersecurity competency objectives. We leave the reader the task of using the NICE Workforce Framework to tailor their cybersecurity awareness and specialized role-based training programs since each organization's training goals and objectives are unique.

NIST Security and Privacy Controls

The NIST Cybersecurity Framework includes a controls document (NIST Special Publication 800-53 Security and Privacy Controls for

A

Competency #1

Skill #1	Skill #2	Skill #3	Knowledge #1	Knowledge #2	Knowledge #3	Knowledge #4

B

Task #1

Skill #1	Skill #2	Skill #3	Knowledge #1	Knowledge #2	Knowledge #3	Knowledge #4

C

Position Description

Competency #1	Competency #2	Competency #3	Competency #4

D

Work Role

Task #1	Task #2	Task #3	Task #4	Task #5

E

Credential

Competency #1	Competency #2	Competency #3	Competency #4	Competency #5

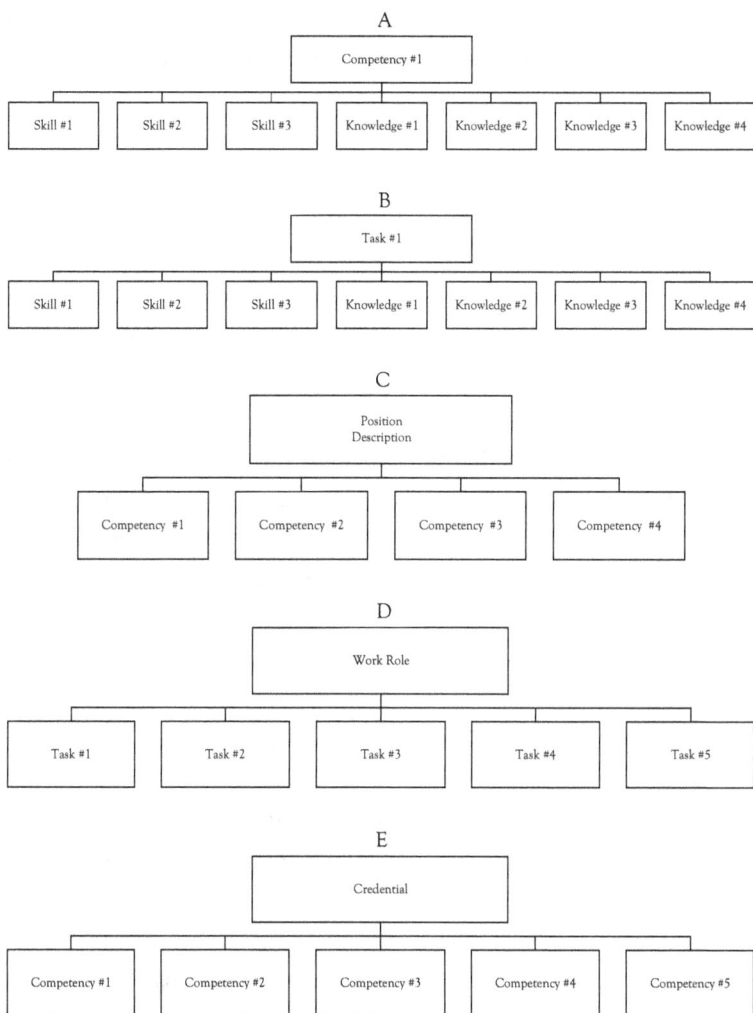

Figure I.10 NICE Workforce Framework

Information Systems and Organizations 2020a) with which organizations can guide their cybersecurity development (e.g., optimization)
and for NIST guidance purposes (Figure I.9). Controls in the NIST
ecosystem are "means of managing risk, including policies, procedures,
guidelines, practices or organizational structures, which can be of an
administrative, technical, management or legal nature" (NIST 2020a,
8). For example, Framework users are guided by the NIST Cybersecurity
Framework controls (NIST 2020a) to establish and maintain policies

and procedures related to cybersecurity, provide training, keep training records, and continually improve the cybersecurity training program through feedback (Figure I.11).

It is against these five training controls that may be evaluated in a NIST cybersecurity audit for the awareness and training category. The training team can leverage the NIST Cybersecurity Framework controls to guide cybersecurity training optimizations:

1. *Policies and procedures*: Develop, document, and disseminate cybersecurity awareness and training policies and procedures. Designate ownership for the policy and review and update the policy and procedures. Policies describe the "what" of cybersecurity, and procedures guide "how" to comply with the cybersecurity policy. Cybersecurity policies and procedures are intended to inform the organization of its security requirements. Cybersecurity awareness and training programs benefit from policies and procedures that reduce risks while achieving learning outcomes. Policies and procedures are standard quality assurance tools used in projects.

2. *Literacy training and awareness*: Provide literacy and awareness training and revise based on feedback, cybersecurity incidents lessons learned, changed regulations, and other inputs. Awareness of security and privacy comes first, followed by understanding security and privacy issues.

3. *Specialized role-based cybersecurity training*: Deliver and update role-based training based on best practices and lessons learned from cybersecurity incidents.

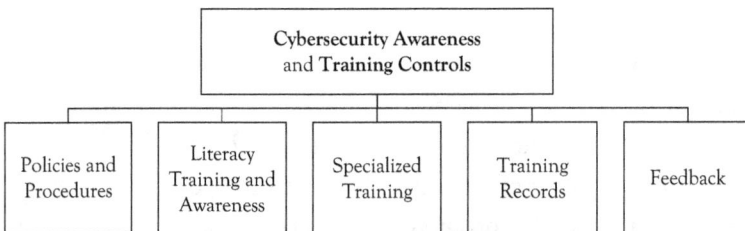

Figure I.11 NIST cybersecurity awareness and training controls

4. *Training records*: Document, monitor, and retain records of training activities, including awareness and specialized training. Training records form the basis for quality improvement programs, and sophisticated AI tools can identify learning gaps and opportunities. LMS increasingly expands data capture and analytics capabilities that transform training records management. LMS are often integrated with other systems like human resources (HRIS), scheduling, and other systems, resulting in more useful training reports.

5. *Feedback*: Leverage learning feedback, especially for critical roles, to take early action (Figure II.22). Feedback (quantitative and/or qualitative) is part of quality management and often appears in this book. We will examine best practices for evaluating learning and demonstrate how to incorporate the Kirkpatrick Model for training evaluation.

The NIST Cybersecurity Framework guides organizations to continually improve these training-related controls (policies and procedures, literacy, awareness and specialized role-based training, training records, and feedback) to improve cybersecurity readiness.

NIST Cybersecurity Framework Summary

The NIST Cybersecurity Framework and family of documents (Table I.4) can guide the training team to plan, develop, implement, and optimize cybersecurity training. They are meant to be tailored and combined to meet the unique needs of the organization.

The NIST Cybersecurity Framework (and supporting documents) is designed to be tailored to the unique needs of organizations:

The Framework should be used in conjunction with other resources to better manage cybersecurity risks. The outcomes are based on and are mapped to existing global standards, guidelines, and practices. Organizations can use the Framework to efficiently scale their cybersecurity programs, address the dynamic and global

Table I.4 NIST training-related documents

NIST document	Training implication
NIST, 2023. *Cybersecurity Framework 2.0,* Initial Public Draft	The top-level cybersecurity framework details the Awareness and Training category and two subcategories: (1) awareness and (2) specialized role-based training.
NIST, 2018. *Framework for Improving Critical Infrastructure Cybersecurity 1.1*	The top-level cybersecurity framework includes the Awareness and Training category and five subcategories: (1) awareness, (2) privileged user, (3) third party, (4) physical and cybersecurity personnel, and (5) senior executive roles.
NICCS: National Initiative for Cybersecurity Careers and Studies, 2022. *The Workforce Framework for Cybersecurity (NICE Framework) Work Roles*	Outlines the 52 work roles (e.g., Systems Administrator and Information Systems Security Manager) divided into seven categories (e.g., Protect and Defend). Identify and prioritize the work roles required for specialized cybersecurity training.
NIST, 2020a Sept. *Special Publication 800-53, Rev. 5: Security and Privacy Controls for Information Systems and Organizations*	Provides a catalog of security and privacy controls to protect the organization from cyber incidents. Controls guide risk prevention and mitigation actions.
NIST, 2003. *Special Publication 800-50: Building an Information Technology Security Awareness and Training Program*	Outlines the components of cybersecurity awareness, training, and education with guidance to plan, develop, and implement these programs.
NIST, 2014. *Special Publication 800-16, Version 1 (3rd Draft): A Role-Based Model for Federal Information Technology/ Cybersecurity Training*	Introduces the Cybersecurity Learning Continuum and guidance to develop, implement, and evaluate role-based cybersecurity training.
NIST, 2020b. *NIST Special Publication 800-181, Rev. 1: Workforce Framework for Cybersecurity (NICE Framework)*	The NICE training "building blocks" include task, knowledge, and skill statements.

nature of cybersecurity risks, and adapt to technological advances and business and legal requirements. The Framework applies to all information and communications technology (ICT), including information technology (IT), the Internet of Things (IoT), and operational technology (OT) used by an organization. It also applies to all types of technology environments, including cloud, mobile, and artificial intelligence systems. The Framework is forward-looking and is intended to apply to future changes in technologies and environments. (NIST 2023, 3)

Thus, users are invited to implement and customize the Framework according to their priorities. The Framework's flexibility and broad applicability are reasons this book aligns with the NIST Cybersecurity Framework for cybersecurity training.

Microlearning

The NIST Cybersecurity Framework is a "living" framework of best practices that will reward the learner with repeat visits to NIST websites.

- Review any of the NIST family of documents that may interest you. There are links to these documents in our References appendix.
- Search for training records management best practices. Use online tools to compare and contrast the NIST Cybersecurity Framework and the ISO/IEC 27000:2018 Information security management systems standard.
- Search for NIST updates; they will provide quantum technology updates with profound training and development implications.
- Sign up for NIST alerts for updates to the NIST Cybersecurity Framework and supporting documents.

NIST Training Continuum

Cybersecurity competence can be illustrated on a NIST Cybersecurity Learning Continuum (Figure I.12), beginning with security awareness, cybersecurity essentials training, cybersecurity specialized role-based training, professional development (certifications), and education (after NIST 2003, 8–10).

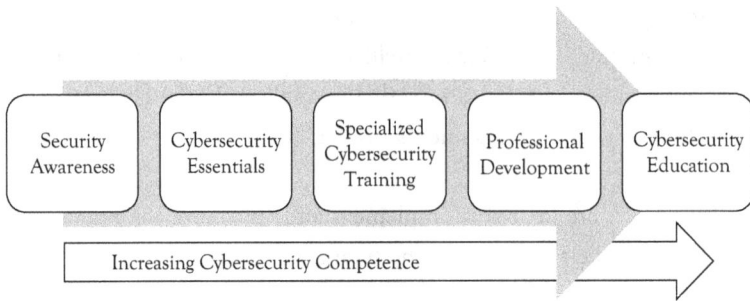

Figure I.12 Cybersecurity Learning Continuum

The NIST Cybersecurity Learning Continuum categorizes the common types of cybersecurity training, and the amount of competence in cybersecurity increases as one progresses from short awareness training courses to degree-granting cybersecurity programs:

- *Security awareness*: Inform the learner of general security concerns (e.g., keeping a tidy desk) to allow all organization members to act appropriately.
- *Cybersecurity essentials*: Provide cybersecurity risk and issue management to help individuals act appropriately. Cybersecurity awareness training often includes elements of security awareness and cybersecurity essentials topics.
- *Specialized cybersecurity training*: Deliver role-based content to build competencies to perform relevant tasks with security risks in mind (e.g., privileged access users, finance personnel, senior leadership, and others who access sensitive business data).
- *Professional development*: Develop advanced professional competencies to perform their roles. The training is often in a specialized field (e.g., cloud security responsibilities) and may include assessment activities. Some professional certifications are nontechnical (e.g., Project Management Professional), while others may be based on proprietary technology (e.g., Microsoft Security Engineer).
- *Education*: Learn in-depth cybersecurity content like training, but education is broader in scope. Often, degree, certificate,

and diploma programs from colleges and universities provide sufficient depth and breadth of content to develop security specialists.[12]

We use the NIST Cybersecurity Learning Continuum in *Cybersecurity Training* to guide our training scope (security awareness, cybersecurity essentials, and specialized training). More advanced training through professional certifications and cybersecurity education is out of our planning, delivery, and evaluation scope. Our scope is security awareness, cybersecurity essentials, and specialized cybersecurity training (Figure I.12). Applying Bloom's Taxonomy guides training and allows innovative practices like simulations to aid learning.

NIST Awareness and Training Program

The cybersecurity awareness training program (NIST 2003) combines NIST security awareness and cybersecurity essentials training content (Figures I.9 and I.12) for employees and third-party stakeholders. For example, the cybersecurity awareness training module may be part of employee onboarding. Learners are introduced to the basics of physical security (e.g., the procedure for a lost key or identification badge) and cybersecurity (e.g., how to spot phishing). Cybersecurity awareness training programs can include content to shape or shift the organization's culture (e.g., "cybersecurity is everyone's responsibility"). General awareness training can reinforce an organization's principles (e.g., focus on value, collaborate, progress iteratively, build quality, etc.). The organization's culture and principles are related, and cybersecurity general awareness training can contribute to cultural transformation (e.g., strengthening cybersecurity readiness). Aldag and his research team (2022, 269) discovered that the learners' behaviors were no longer significantly better than before the training experience six to eight

---

[12] Education and professional development for cybersecurity professionals was addressed in *Shields Up: Cybersecurity Project Management*, where education and professional development trends and opportunities were detailed with the goal of assisting in the reader's professional development.

months after cybersecurity training. One concludes that training must be ongoing to maintain appropriate cybersecurity readiness behaviors, especially when the threats are ever-changing. The learner may receive specialized training (e.g., privileged user or physical security guard roles) if the person has a crucial role in cybersecurity.

NIST Specialized Training

The NIST (2023) Cybersecurity Framework includes the specialized (role-based) training subcategory in the Protect cybersecurity function (Table I.3). Organizations seeking more guidance about role-based training can review the NIST (2014) *A Role-Based Model for Federal Information Technology/Cybersecurity Training* document (Figure I.9). Four common IT security roles are identified that can benefit from specialized cybersecurity training:

1. Privileged users: IT specialists who can modify systems, logs, user accounts, data files, and system applications.
2. Third-party users: customers, suppliers, and partners.
3. Senior leaders: leadership and board-level leadership.
4. Physical and cybersecurity personnel: security guards and cybersecurity specialists.

Since there are hundreds of IT roles in organizations, instructional designers combine roles for specialized training. For example, the Incident Response and Handling role includes recommended skills and knowledge (Figure I.13) that can be mapped to roles such as the System Administrator and Incident Responder. Since the NIST Cybersecurity Framework no longer lists specific roles (e.g., privileged users) and instead uses the "specialized roles" terminology, organizations can more easily apply the framework. Therefore, the organization can identify which categories and subcategories in the NIST Cybersecurity Framework to improve. If training is required, they can use the NIST *A Role-Based Model for Federal Information Technology/Cybersecurity Training* document to identify and prioritize role areas and roles for training development (Figure I.9). Bundling roles and categorization can help

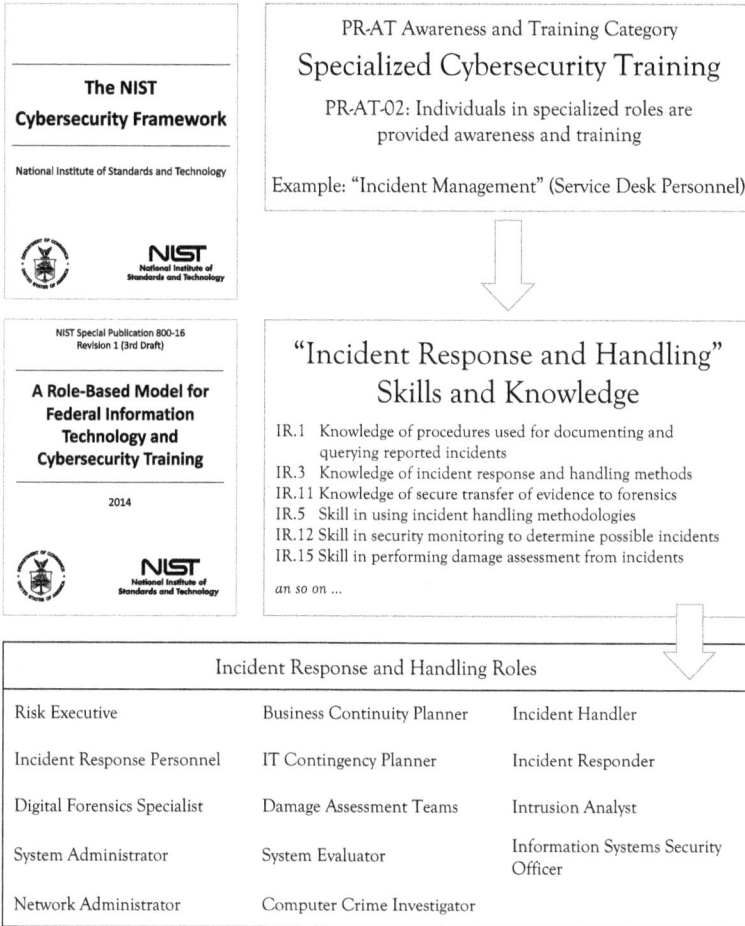

The NIST
Cybersecurity Framework

National Institute of Standards and Technology

NIST
National Institute of
Standards and Technology

PR-AT Awareness and Training Category

Specialized Cybersecurity Training

PR-AT-02: Individuals in specialized roles are
provided awareness and training

Example: "Incident Management" (Service Desk Personnel)

NIST Special Publication 800-16
Revision 1 (3rd Draft)

A Role-Based Model for
Federal Information
Technology and
Cybersecurity Training

2014

NIST
National Institute of
Standards and Technology

"Incident Response and Handling" Skills and Knowledge

IR.1   Knowledge of procedures used for documenting and
         querying reported incidents
IR.3   Knowledge of incident response and handling methods
IR.11 Knowledge of secure transfer of evidence to forensics
IR.5   Skill in using incident handling methodologies
IR.12 Skill in security monitoring to determine possible incidents
IR.15 Skill in performing damage assessment from incidents

an so on ...

Incident Response and Handling Roles

Risk Executive	Business Continuity Planner	Incident Handler
Incident Response Personnel	IT Contingency Planner	Incident Responder
Digital Forensics Specialist	Damage Assessment Teams	Intrusion Analyst
System Administrator	System Evaluator	Information Systems Security Officer
Network Administrator	Computer Crime Investigator	

Figure I.13 NIST specialized role-based training

the organization reduce the number of roles that require training (again, the Goldilocks approach).

A person will perform in a position (e.g., Incident Response Personnel) but may be assigned multiple roles (e.g., Incident Handler, Intrusion Analyst, Digital Forensics Specialist, and Computer Crime Investigator). A person may perform informal roles like being a communications facilitator among the project stakeholders or the green solution champion. The project sponsor usually manages, funds, and supports the overall project but is less involved with day-to-day activities. The project sponsor is accountable for benefits realization of the digital product or service delivered through the project delivery approach. The project sponsor is ideally a servant leader who helps project teams succeed. Therefore, one position may encapsulate multiple roles. The instructional designer can bundle NIST roles (tailoring and combining) to reduce the number of specialized training modules (later described in the Box Car approach, Figure II.11).

The knowledge and skills developed in cybersecurity awareness and specialized training can be maintained in many ways, such as by creating a community of practice. Communities of practice form and meet regularly to learn about a topic of interest like cybersecurity. There can be synergies in motivated groups, and communities of practice are growing in numbers and diversity.[13] These are best led from the "bottom" rather than the "top" (e.g., managers). A cybersecurity community of practice can guide cybersecurity awareness and specialized training; democratization of training and learning improves engagement and outcomes attainment. Many look beyond the classroom approach to develop and maintain competence and may use gamification, leaderboards, and awards to measure and reward ongoing learning (e.g., getting ready for quantum technologies and use cases).

Since tailoring and combining are training design best practices, we recommend the reader review these NIST Cybersecurity Framework documents outlined in *Cybersecurity Training* to improve their understanding of the NIST training approach. The "References" section in the appendixes includes links to these free online resources (Figure I.9).

Microlearning

You can find out more about NIST cybersecurity training online:

- How are NIST communities of practice organized?
- What are the top cybersecurity professional development certifications and advanced education programs?
- Are there recent NIST training updates?

---

[13] The author has formed two communities of practice: The Abu Dhabi Oriental Carpet Group to learn about and enjoy oriental carpets and weavings, and later the Bond University Gamification Community of Practice to learn about and conduct research about serious games and gamification.

ISO/IEC 27000:2018 Information Security Management Systems

Another global cybersecurity standard is ISO/IEC 27000:2018—Information technology—Security techniques—Information security management systems—Overview and vocabulary (often shortened to ISO/IEC 27000). Like the NIST Cybersecurity Framework, it is a set of cybersecurity policies and processes applicable to any industry of any size. The ISO/IEC 27000 is like an overview of the series of standards, including ISO/IEC 27001 Information security management systems (initiate, implement, maintain, and improve security). Since ISO/IEC 27000 has "information" in its title, there are three goals related to protecting the organization's information and achieving the right amount of information: (1) availability, (2) integrity, and (3) confidentiality.

A critical difference between the NIST Cybersecurity Framework and the ISO/IEC 27000 standards is an organization can become certified in ISO/IEC 27000. ISO/IEC 27000 certification signifies the organization's people, processes, and technologies follow best practices in information security. While the NIST Cybersecurity Framework includes an audit process and tiers to guide continual improvement, one does not get certified in the NIST Cybersecurity Framework. To get ISO/IEC 27000 certified, one goes through a certification process and provides evidence of information security best practices, including cybersecurity training (ISO/IEC 27001:2022, Clause 7.3 Awareness).

In this book, we align with the NIST Cybersecurity Framework rather than ISO/IEC 27000 since NIST has extensive training-related resources freely available to support cybersecurity readiness. However, the principles, processes, and tools (e.g., ADDIE Instructional Design, Bloom's Taxonomy, and Kirkpatrick Evaluation Model) in *Cybersecurity Training* apply to ISO cybersecurity and other standards and frameworks where cybersecurity training is required.

While there is advice online to guide the user in selecting the best security standards and frameworks for their organization, the decision may be guided by the ecosystem in which one participates. For example, a medical device vendor selling into the American market may align with the NIST Cybersecurity Framework as it is more prevalent than

ISO/IEC 27000. However, if an engineering consultancy provides services to a European public service agency, they may select ISO/IEC 27000 since it is more prevalent in Europe than NIST. Indeed, many Fortune 500 organizations are certified in ISO/IEC 27000 and align with NIST requirements since they have an international presence.

Microlearning

While *Cybersecurity Training* uses the NIST Cybersecurity Framework to anchor cybersecurity training, the ISO/IEC 27000 standard is also popular:

- Search for which is better, NIST or ISO cybersecurity?
- How long does it take to get ISO/IEC 27000 certified?
- What are the benefits of ISO/IEC 27000 maturity?

Project Management Frameworks

Cybersecurity projects, including training, can benefit from a lean project management approach; that is, apply, tailor, and combine project management tools and processes to cybersecurity training to improve the probability of success. There is a continuum of project management approaches ranging from traditional to adaptive project delivery approaches.

Hybrid Project Management

Hybrid project management adds adaptive, tailoring, and combining techniques to the traditional or waterfall delivery approach (Figure I.14). When technology is delivered, a transition to production (T2P) phase is included to prepare the new digital product (e.g., collaborative robotics manufacturing) or service (e.g., new software or training) for use by the organization. The final tasks required to bring the digital products or services to the end users are critical, ranging from training the service desk team to completing the final technical tasks like penetration testing. The project's product or service is handed over to the sponsor and end user to derive value. We are guided by lean project management, where we

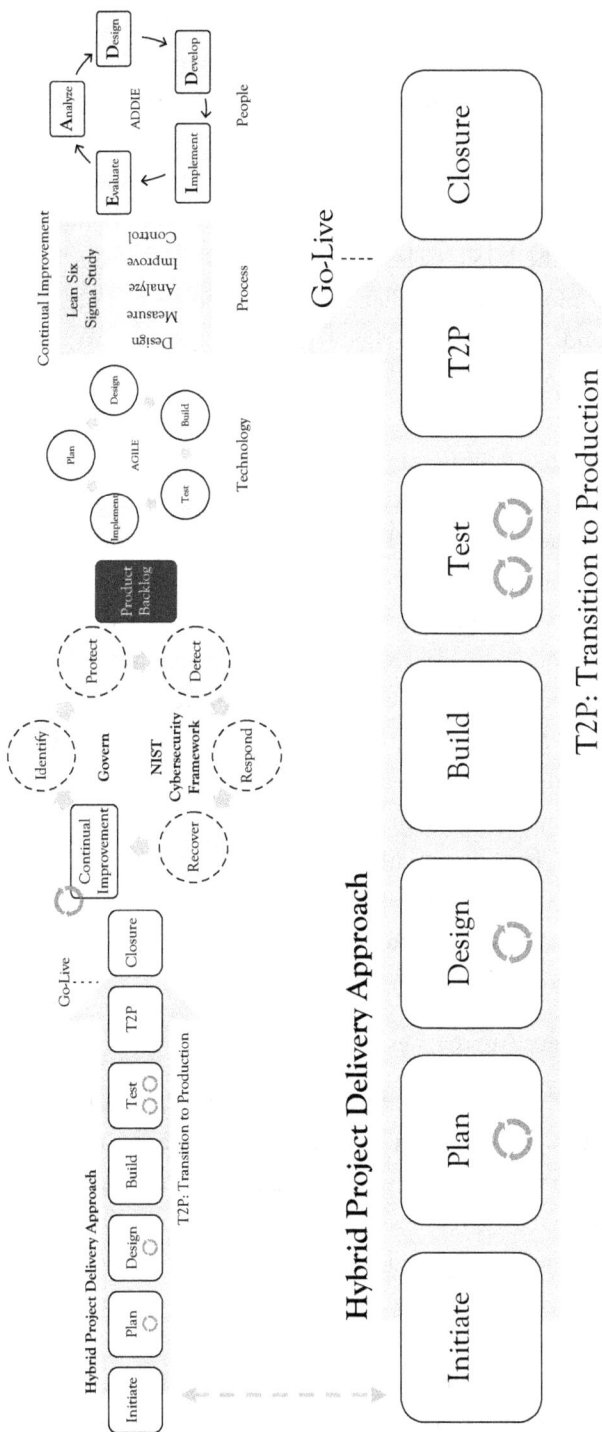

Hybrid Project Delivery Approach

T2P: Transition to Production

Figure I.14 Hybrid project delivery approach

implement "minimum viable products and services" or basic versions that meet the prioritized needs of the end users (also known as the "vanilla" or "Goldilocks" version). We then collect requests for further development and optimization.

We use the hybrid project delivery approach to implement most cybersecurity technologies most of the time. Cybersecurity includes six functions from the NIST Cybersecurity Framework that can be delivered through projects and smaller initiatives: govern, identify, protect, detect, respond, and recover (Figure I.15). In *Cybersecurity Training*, we combine continual improvement (ISO 9001) practices with the NIST cybersecurity functions. Continual improvement is the process of planning, implementing, monitoring, and correcting any defects in the quality management systems (or taking proactive action to improve cybersecurity readiness). The IT security team applies these functions in the production environment (also known as the operational or live environment). They will use the cybersecurity software and request new functionality or optimizations to improve their cybersecurity capabilities. These requests are managed, prioritized, and approved through the ITIL Service Request Management practice. Once approved, the new functionality is scheduled for implementation through a significant project (Figure I.14) or an optimization sprint or initiative (Figure I.16).

There is no cybersecurity without projects; organizations cannot buy cybersecurity at their favorite online retailer or corner store. Therefore, project management is critical to cybersecurity.

Adaptive Delivery Approaches

Adaptive project delivery approaches (agile, Kanban, etc.) have gained popularity and are increasingly used among their early adopters: the information technology industry, including software engineering. Adaptive project delivery approaches can improve the probability of project success when there is change and ambiguity. In *Cybersecurity Training*, we use adaptive delivery approaches to optimize digital products and services like cybersecurity operations and training (Figure I.16).

Organizations can use the hybrid project delivery approach to deliver the minimum viable cybersecurity product or service. The IT

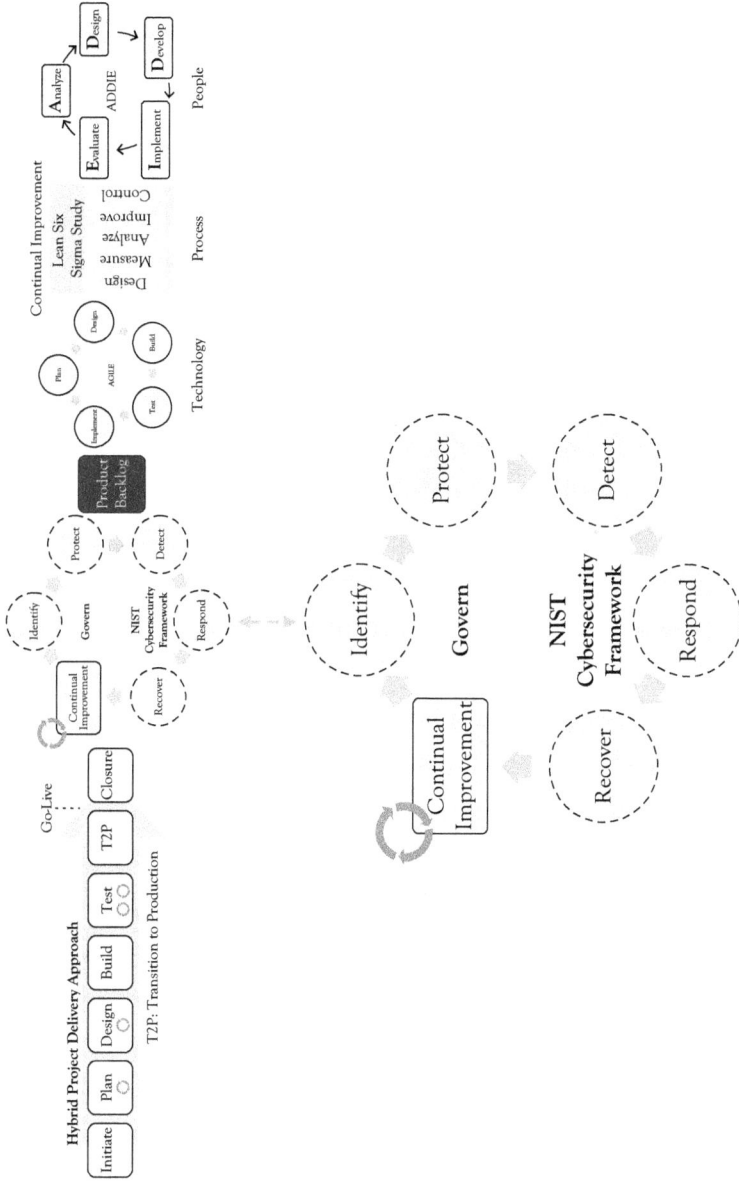

Figure I.15 Cybersecurity Framework with continual improvement

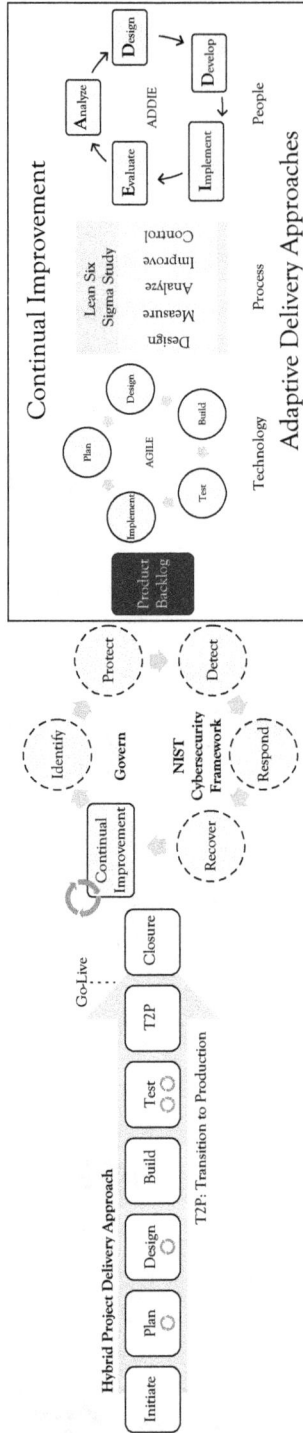

Figure I.16 Optimization sprints—people, process, and technology

security team uses the new product or service and requests improvements (e.g., increased automation). Practitioners may use adaptive delivery approaches to optimize cybersecurity: agile project management (technologies), Lean Six Sigma (processes), and the ADDIE Model of Instructional Design (people—competencies).

Agile Project Management: Technology

After cybersecurity (or any other technology) has been implemented, end users often request improvements or enhancements. For example, an IT cybersecurity supervisor may request a technology enhancement to activate advanced cybersecurity detection functions built into their software. Large-scale improvements can be delivered with hybrid project management (Figure I.14), while minor optimizations (initiatives) can be implemented through adaptive delivery sprints (Figure I.16).

Teams can use agile scrums to optimize technology like cybersecurity applications (Figure I.17). Adaptive project delivery approaches like agile scrums are helpful when there are requirements, process, or technology ambiguities. Agile project delivery is a common approach to continually improve technology once it has been implemented and used by the organization (e.g., cybersecurity). We add lessons learned activities (sprint review and retrospective) to the agile sprints. Since we invite the reader to tailor and combine, your adaptive project management approach may differ. Other sources have explained agile project management (Schwaber and Sutherland 2017; Skulmoski 2022), and we will rely on the reader to review adaptive project management approaches if required.

We emphasize that product backlogs are heterogeneous that can include optimization requests for technologies, processes, and people (Figure I.16). The product backlog includes technical requirements like adding additional integration (agile approach) and nontechnical requirements like removing pain points from a process (Lean Six Sigma approach) or providing new cybersecurity training (ADDIE Model approach). Therefore, the overall product backlog will have a mix of prioritized requirements to optimize the digital product or service: people, processes, and technologies. Often, systems optimization projects come with a training requirement.

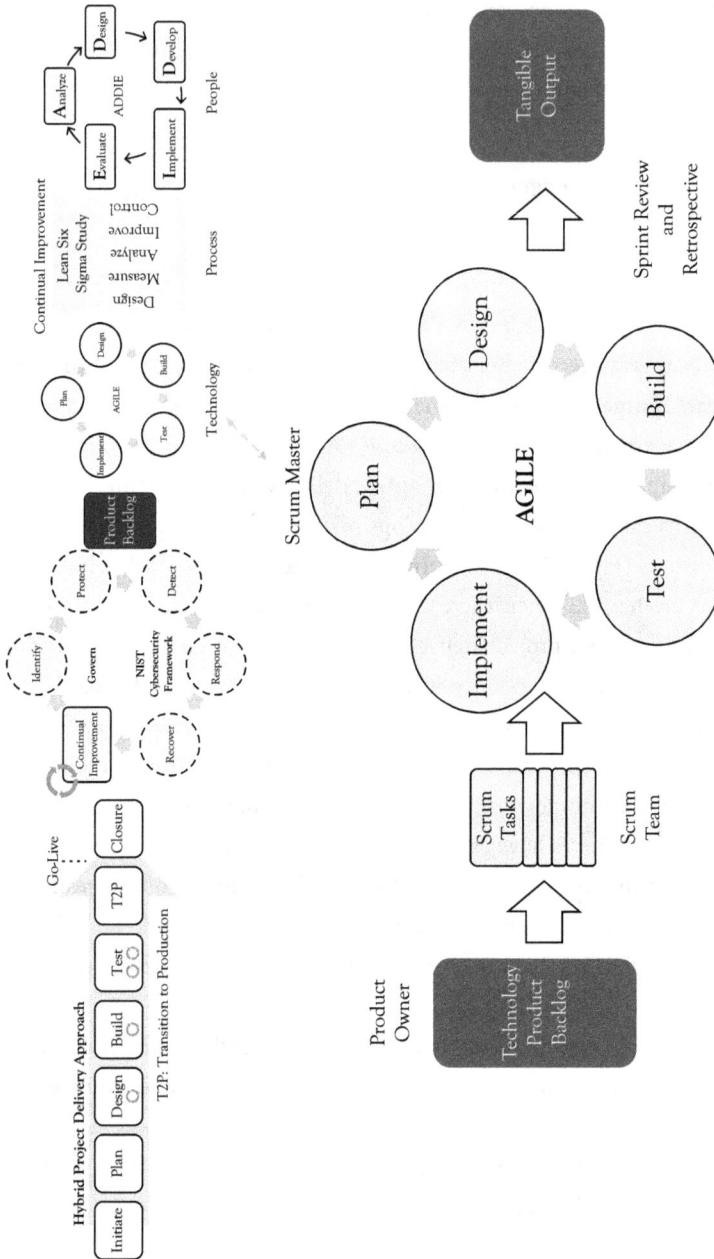

Figure 1.17 Agile project delivery approach—technology

Following the Agile Manifesto is a critical success factor for agile and other adaptive project techniques; indeed, the Agile Manifesto also applies to the hybrid project delivery approach. The Agile Manifesto includes 4 principles and 12 values (Figure I.18). The Agile Manifesto is the companion to the agile scrum delivery method; agile scrums are more likely to be successful when the Agile Manifesto guides the team. Values are standards of behavior that are subjective and may change over time. We use values to make decisions about what is right and wrong.

Principles are like rules and are permanent. The Agile Manifesto principles apply to all agile projects; principles are unchanging. We revised two principles where we substituted the delivery of working software for deliverables for delivery of value. Our modification broadens the applicability of the Agile Manifesto beyond software development to any technology project. Indeed, our modified Agile Manifesto can be

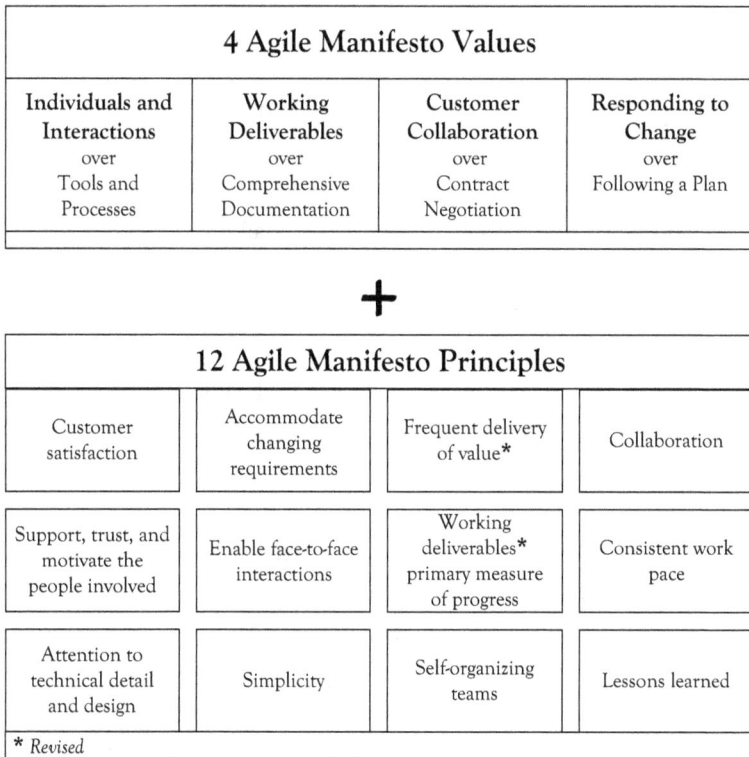

4 Agile Manifesto Values			
Individuals and Interactions	Working Deliverables	Customer Collaboration	Responding to Change
over	over	over	over
Tools and Processes	Comprehensive Documentation	Contract Negotiation	Following a Plan

+

12 Agile Manifesto Principles			
Customer satisfaction	Accommodate changing requirements	Frequent delivery of value*	Collaboration
Support, trust, and motivate the people involved	Enable face-to-face interactions	Working deliverables* primary measure of progress	Consistent work pace
Attention to technical detail and design	Simplicity	Self-organizing teams	Lessons learned
* Revised			

Figure I.18 Revised Agile Manifesto

applied to nontechnical projects like training projects using the ADDIE Model of Instructional Design. Reviewing our generalized Agile Manifesto will show the values and principles that apply to ADDIE training projects if we take a general view and replace "delivering software" with "working deliverables."

Agile-delivered projects often struggle not due to the delivery approach; agile projects often fail because not enough of the Agile Manifesto was applied. In *Cybersecurity Training*, we recommend following the Agile Manifesto's values and principles in cybersecurity training and other training projects. We combine the hybrid project delivery approach, adding adaptive iterations as required (e.g., project managers may follow an iterative approach in the design phase to arrive at an approved design). A practitioner might adopt the principles and values of the Agile Manifesto, whether they use a traditional, agile, or hybrid project delivery approach.

Microlearning

Increasingly, adaptive project delivery methods are used, resulting in many online resources:

- Search for which is better: agile or waterfall project management?
- When should agile project management be used?
- What is the most surprising application of agile? For example, how is agile project management used in the museum industry?

Lean Six Sigma: Process

IT security teams might use the Lean Six Sigma approach (Figure I.19) to improve cybersecurity (e.g., recovery procedures) or other IT processes (e.g., incident resolution procedures). The Lean Six Sigma process brings together lean and the Six Sigma problem-solving approaches to improve process performance (e.g., throughput) by reducing/eliminating waste (lean) and reducing process variation (Six Sigma). Many digital transformation projects have process improvement goals, and the Lean Six Sigma

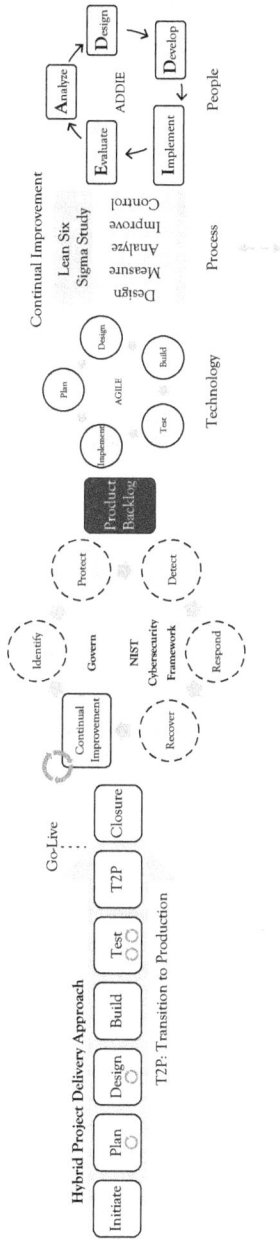

Hybrid Project Delivery Approach

Initiate | Plan | Design | Build | Test | T2P | Closure

Go-Live

T2P: Transition to Production

Continual Improvement

ADDIE: Analyze, Design, Develop, Implement, Evaluate — People

Lean Six Sigma Study: Design, Measure, Analyze, Improve, Control — Process

Plan, Design, Build, Test — AGILE — Technology

Product Backlog

NIST Cybersecurity Framework: Govern, Identify, Protect, Detect, Respond, Recover

Continual Improvement

Lean Six Sigma

1. Define	2. Measure	3. Analyze	4. Improve	5. Control
Develop a project charter: 1. Business case 2. Problem statement 3. Scope 4. Resources 5. Schedule 6. Project benefits	Measure the "process variables" (e.g., turnaround time) and collect baseline data. Compare final performance to this baseline data.	Conduct a root cause analysis (RCA). Verify and validate root causes.	Develop solutions to root causes to improve the process. Design, build and test the solutions. Refine and implement the solution.	Monitor process performance after implementing the improvements and compare the new measurements to baseline data.
Business Project	Business Problem Solving		Technology Project	Operations Management

Known as DMAIC (dee-may-ic) in lean Six Sigma vocabulary

Figure I.19 Lean Six Sigma—process

approach can be helpful during the design phase to transform the legacy process. The Lean Six Sigma problem-solving approach is process-based: define the project, measure to create a baseline, analyze the problem, improve by implementing the solution, and monitor and control the process to determine if waste and process variation are reduced.

Business units (e.g., pharmacy operations, engineering, accounts payable, manufacturing, etc.) often develop strategic plans to improve their processes. They may undertake a Lean Six Sigma improvement project, and in the "improve" phase, they may request technology to automate steps in their process or to integrate systems. Therefore, their process improvement project may require a technology project (e.g., digital transformation to automate steps in the process) to deliver the improved process (Figure I.19). Practitioners can follow the hybrid project delivery approach (tailoring and combining) to provide DMAIC-based improvement. New processes often require new training in the process or supporting technologies.

Microlearning

The Lean Six Sigma problem-solving approach is popular for improving business processes. There are many online resources, including free Lean Six Sigma training:

- What are Lean Six Sigma best practices?
- What are Lean Six Sigma implementation risks?
- What are Lean Six Sigma use cases and success stories?
- What Lean Six Sigma tools and templates are available?

ADDIE Model of Instructional Design: People

Organizations can use ADDIE sprints (analyze, design, develop, implement, and evaluate training) to improve an organization's people capabilities (Figure I.20).

Later in *Cybersecurity Training*, we present a project-oriented approach to deliver cybersecurity training based on the ADDIE Model of Instructional Design.

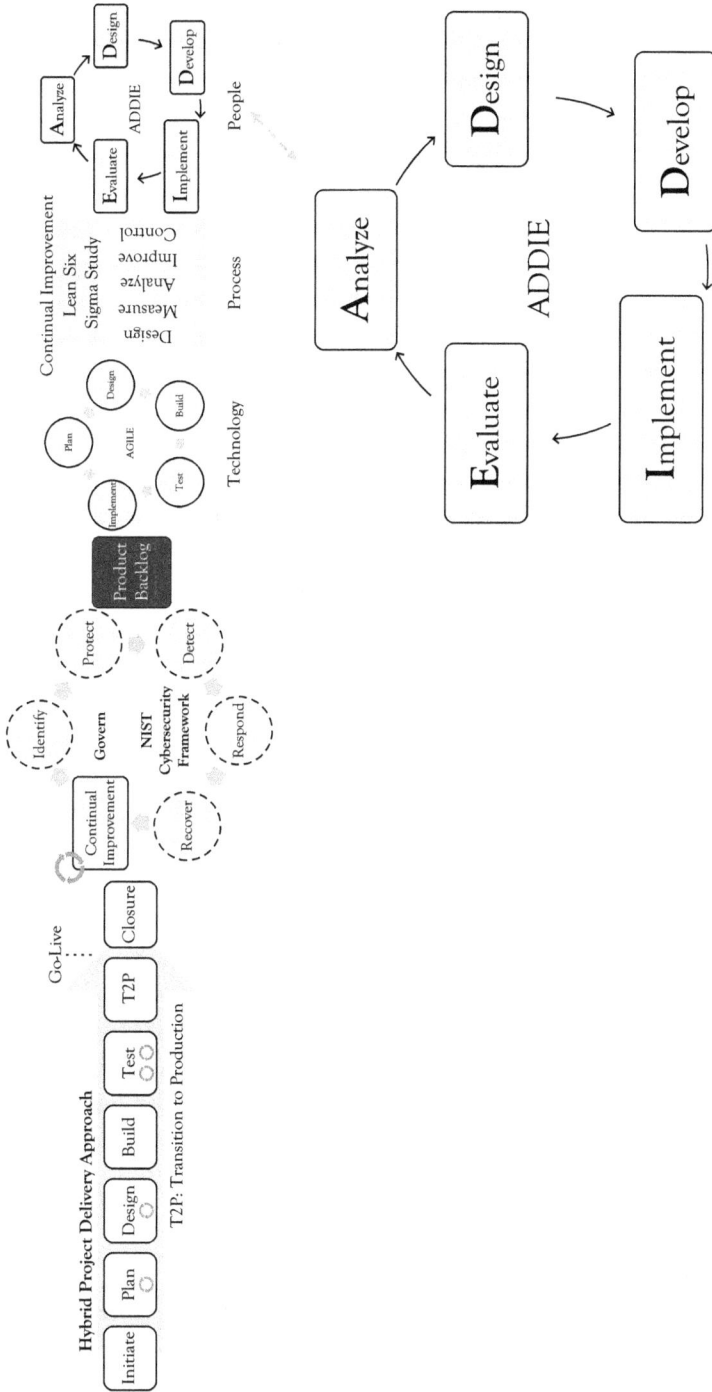

Figure I.20 ADDIE Model of Instructional Design—people

Thus, we tailor the classic project delivery approach to cybersecurity capabilities and combine adaptive approaches to optimize people, processes, and technologies to increase value. Without project management, implementing and optimizing cybersecurity would be highly challenging.

Managing Training Projects to Frameworks

Aligning work to standards like the Guide to the Project Management Body of Knowledge and frameworks like the National Institute of Standards and Technology Cybersecurity Framework improves the probability of project success (Figure I.21). The fundamental value proposition of frameworks and standards is that they can improve quality and reduce risks if appropriately applied, tailored, and combined.

In this book, we align with leading standards, frameworks, and models that are globally adopted. To deliver cybersecurity projects, we align with the Project Management Body of Knowledge from the Project Management Institute. The PMBOK® Guide aligns with ISO risk and quality management best practices. We use the NIST Cybersecurity Framework since it applies to most organizations in most industries and is freely available, albeit without a certification pathway. Our technology continual improvement efforts in *Cybersecurity Training* align with agile project delivery. We use Lean Six Sigma to improve processes and the ADDIE Model of Instructional Design to improve people's capabilities through training. Since cybersecurity includes a collection of digital technologies, we align with ITIL digital service management. Therefore, in *Cybersecurity Training*, we combine and follow standards to provide a pathway to cybersecurity readiness.

Cybersecurity Training and Learning Ecosystem

In *Cybersecurity Training*, we take a systems approach to project management, cybersecurity, and training, combining the most relevant and valuable components into a holistic learning ecosystem. Our ecosystem is supported by the classic pillars of people, process, and technology that allow tailoring, especially in times of change (e.g., VUCA environment: volatility, uncertainty, complexity, and ambiguity). We add good

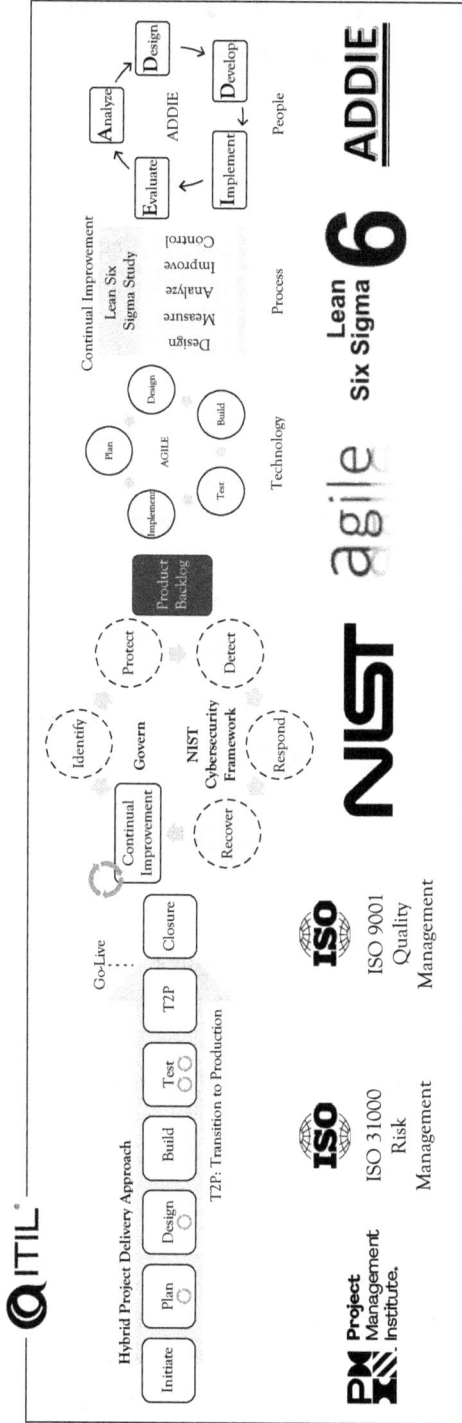

Figure 1.21 Standards and frameworks alignment

governance practices (aligned with ITIL and the PMBOK® Guide), such as developing and reviewing the learning ecosystem's vision, principles, and objectives.

Vision, Principles, Goals, and Objectives

Learning ecosystems can be shaped through leadership, who communicates and demonstrates the learning ecosystem's desired vision, principles, and objectives.

Vision

Good governance includes the vision for the learning ecosystem (e.g., target state). The vision is an image of what the ecosystem will look like, such as a state of readiness. Thought leaders outline their direction (e.g., a strategic plan and purpose) to motivate their team and other stakeholders, for example:

- Optimize our human capabilities while providing balance.
- Develop cybersecurity readiness capabilities across the organization and supply chain.
- Create a learning ecosystem that encourages lifelong and ubiquitous learning.

Significant change is occurring in learning, and you may already follow trends in training, learning, LMS, and implementing elements of the emerging metaverse. We predict innovations in cybersecurity training, incident response playbook practice, and simulations in the metaverse. All delivered through projects!

Principles

We see principles as rules that guide behavior; they prescribe what we should do. Take a moment to review the principles from the Project Management Institute, agile project delivery (scrum), and ITIL. You will see the easy alignment of their core value propositions: follow our approach to improve the probability of delivering the right quality

Table I.5 Tailor and combine principles

Principle	Source
Focus on value	ITIL
Collaborate and promote visibility	ITIL
Build-in quality into processes	PMI
Tailor based on context	PMI
Organize for a consistent work pace	Agile
Accommodate changing requirements	Agile
Etc.	–

while minimizing risks. Since the value proposition of these standards, frameworks, and models are similar, a natural alignment underlies them. Instructional designers can combine and tailor these principles in our learning ecosystem. You may review these principles and tailor them to your learning ecosystem and projects (Table I.5).

Principles are more readily adopted when they are lived by leaders, especially when they follow the principles even in challenging circumstances.

Goals and Objectives

Goals are broad outcomes achieved through the organization's activities. Goals are not easily measured. For example, the project sponsor may identify improving cybersecurity readiness as a broad goal, including the readiness of people, technologies, and systems. How can cybersecurity readiness be measured? We use project management techniques in *Cybersecurity Training* to break down the readiness goals into measurable operational objectives. For example, the training team may track the number of IT team members who complete online CSIRT respond and recover playbook simulations.

Objectives are measurable achievements (e.g., a project) the organization or team plan and achieve. Objectives are diverse and may be financial (revenue- and cost-related), performance, operational, customer satisfaction, employee engagement, and so on. Objectives are short-term outcomes. Cybersecurity awareness and specialized training are recurring activities that can contribute to achieving cybersecurity-related KPIs (e.g., preventing successful phishing attacks by 10 percent for the new fiscal year).

Cybersecurity readiness is increasingly essential to organizations globally and across all industries and disciplines. Cybersecurity readiness is when the organization (people, process, and technology) can identify, protect, detect, respond, and recover from cybersecurity incidents and leverage opportunities. Therefore, we predict a continued emphasis on the long-term goal of cybersecurity readiness; indeed, cybersecurity awareness and training are becoming cybersecurity readiness critical success factors (Figure I.1).

People and the Training Organization

Training is part of human resources management and is considered one of its core functions, beginning with acquiring talent:

- *Recruitment and selection*: To bring talent into the organization, human resource professionals follow a process that may involve writing job descriptions and requirements, establishing the salary, advertising, screening, interviewing, and selecting the best candidate. This process may also be known as talent acquisition, culminating in the new hire being onboarded into the organization.
- *Training and development*: As part of onboarding, new hires often receive an orientation to the organization and their home unit. The LMS can support this process. Onboarding training addresses competency deficits while development is broader and ongoing, including mentoring and secondments. The training team may have specialists in LMS to support end users and optimize current systems. The training unit often develops compliance-related content (e.g., health and safety and code of conduct training) delivered online through the LMS. They collaborate widely to develop cybersecurity learning experiences with IT security and other subject matter experts (e.g., with the supply chain and finance units to develop business continuity procedures).

- *Performance management*: With the help of line managers, employees' quality of work, achievements, attitude, effectiveness, and efficiency are assessed regularly and periodically. Depending on the organization's maturity level, periodic performance reviews may include discussions about learning plans, sometimes described as individual development plans. Higher maturity organizations will ensure that strategic learning topics are built into these individual development plans (IDP). An IDP is usually more than simply compliance with mandatory annual training; on the contrary, a well-designed IDP is designed to carry the individual and the organization to a new level. Given the increasing importance of cybersecurity, cybersecurity learning will undoubtedly be a part of many IDPs.

This book is designed for all stakeholders interested in improving its people's cybersecurity capabilities, whether they are trainers within the human resources department or elsewhere in the organization.

Training Technologies

Training technologies help deliver and track the training and development process. They are continually evolving, maturing, and providing innovative opportunities. Therefore, we will avoid comments on specific technologies and look at the critical functions of LMS we use in the training and development process. In *Cybersecurity Training*, we focus on training and leave human resource development to other authorities. We use the ADDIE Model of Instructional Design to analyze training requirements, design and develop training, and implement and evaluate training. We configure our LMS to support the ADDIE Model of Instructional Design process and other functions like training documentation. LMS helps us develop, train, and report on training and learning, a helpful tool as cybersecurity training compliance becomes more prevalent. We have used LMS for over

25 years and have seen maturity in ease of use and expanded functionality like:

- *Integration*: Increasingly, LMS are integrated with other
  systems like content repositories and subscriptions,
  leaderboards, reporting tools, customer relationship
  management systems (CRM), videoconferencing,
  collaboration tools, and so on. Technology optimization
  sprints can add these integration opportunities incrementally
  (e.g., through scrums, Figure I.17).
- *Learning experience platforms*: A learning experience platform
  adds a more appealing user interface and integrates with the
  LMS. Learning Experience Platforms (LXPs) focus on the
  User Experience (UX), providing visually appealing and easy-
  to-use portals. Users can find learning opportunities, display
  learning progress (often with pointsification), and entice the
  learner to complete more learning by showing them their
  progress toward goals, such as digital badges. LXPs can also
  consolidate external learning catalog subscriptions alongside
  an organization's internally hosted LMS content.
- *Learner tracking*: Instructional designers can track, document,
  and analyze the learner's journey individually and collectively
  to better understand training and learner performance. As
  organizations learn more about their people, they will be able
  to support their professional growth in improved ways.
- *Automated alerts*: Instructional designers and managers can
  set up alerts to push notifications to the learner to complete
  assigned training (e.g., health and safety or cybersecurity role-
  based training). We have also set up alerts to notify learners of
  successful learning (e.g., they are at the top of the leaderboard)
  or that new learning resources are available. We notify learners
  of new learning opportunities using LMS (e.g., "Introduction
  to CSIRT for Nontechnical Participants").
- *Reporting and analytics*: Organizations use reporting and
  analytics throughout the training process for evidence-based
  decision making about the efficiency and effectiveness of

their training programs. We expect growth and maturity in reporting and analytics functionality in emerging LMS.

- *Remote-friendly LMS*: LMS functionality is expanding beyond the desktop to mobile and wearable devices. Remote workers can access their LMS accounts wherever they are and with their chosen devices. Remote-friendly learning content may include audiobooks, videos, and snackable content suitable to be accessed via mobile devices. A remote-friendly LMS allows ubiquitous learning for on-the-go workers like those in construction, health care, and emergency services.

- *Assessment tools*: Most LMS can support learning assessments (pretraining, formative, and summative) with different methods like true and false statements (we avoid these as guessing can lead to invalid assessments), multiple choice, branching scenarios, simulations, Likert, and matching questions. Assessment is the data collection process, and evaluation is the analysis of learner performance. While short-answer question development is a core LMS functionality, we caution the user that short-answer questions often require time-intensive manual evaluation. Manual scoring can bring reliability issues and correct mistakes even with well-designed rubrics (see Learning Evaluation Scope). We use automated scoring where possible, especially cybersecurity awareness training because it involves lower rather than higher-level thought and concepts requiring manual evaluation (see Bloom's Taxonomy). We anticipate advances in AI to automate the evaluation of open-ended questions.

- *Learner personalization*: More LMS provide the user with personalization functionality to assist learning and professional development. For example, the user can enroll in training tracks and subscribe to learning that is part of their professional development plan. Automation capabilities will bring learning opportunities to the learner. LXPs typify learner personalization.

- *Centralized learning materials*: Learning repositories (including serious games and simulations) will be broadly available by a subscription or instructional designer-developed learning resources. Analytics can be applied to understand the types of content learners value.

- *Scheduling tools*: LMS may have sophisticated scheduling functionality to optimize training opportunities per learners' schedules. Content delivery can be automated and delivered according to a schedule (e.g., receive an e-mail and link to complete a monthly cybersecurity five-question quiz).
- *Compliance*: LMS can provide evidence to support compliance with external bodies like government, insurance, and partners that the organization has a robust NIST-aligned cybersecurity awareness program.

While LMS is necessary for training success, they are insufficient; we plan and provide training according to best practices outlined in the ADDIE Model of Instructional Design.

Microlearning

Learning technologies will evolve and bring innovations as we see with other technologies. Therefore, monitoring learning technologies online will keep you current on these innovations and plan for future training projects:

- Search for the top LMS.
- Find or generate LMS buyer's guides.
- Search for "Learning Records Store," "Learning Catalogue," "Learning Content Management System," and "Learning Experience Platform." How do these different components differ from and interact with LMS?
- Investigate the metaverse learning and development to gain insight into new training functionalities and use cases.

Part I Conclusion

Cybersecurity awareness and training are an integral part of a cybersecurity ecosystem. A casual observer sees a steady increase in cybersecurity incidents globally, domestically, and locally. There is also an increased response from governments, regulators, agencies, businesses, organizations, and citizens to become more cybersafe. Organizations are implementing projects to improve cybersecurity readiness, leverage opportunities (e.g., "you can trust us with your digital information"), and respond to threats with robust resilience. Organizations develop and maintain cybersecurity readiness through continual improvement of people, processes, and technology and are guided by relevant standards that embody best practices.

Cybersecurity readiness can be achieved by building, maintaining, and optimizing a robust technology platform guided by technology management frameworks like ITIL 4 and COBIT. Organizations build and optimize their cybersecurity ecosystem through projects and rely on best practices outlined in project management delivery standards and frameworks like the PMBOK® Guide and adaptive delivery approaches like agile and hybrid project management. They adopt and align with relevant cybersecurity frameworks like the NIST Cybersecurity Framework or the ISO/IEC 27000 Information security management standard. While organizations traditionally use project management tools and techniques to deliver and improve cybersecurity capabilities (e.g., detect and respond), they apply project management to plan, implement, deliver, and optimize cybersecurity training. Indeed, the project management and training processes are naturally aligned because they both begin with a demand for a product or service, followed by the development and delivery of value. Organizations improve the likelihood of developing and maintaining a robust cybersecurity ecosystem by following a project management approach to deliver cybersecurity awareness and training. Cybersavvy people are a critical success factor that can only be achieved through a robust training program detailed in PART II: Cybersecurity Training.

PART II

Cybersecurity Training

In PART II, we combine cybersecurity project management and related best practices (e.g., PMBOK® Guide, ITIL, ISO risk and quality management, and the NIST Cybersecurity Framework) with training best practices (e.g., ADDIE Model of Instructional Design, Bloom's Taxonomy, and Kirkpatrick Model of Evaluation). We observed when organizations bring together best practices (combining) and choose the elements to fit their unique training project (tailoring), as outlined in *Cybersecurity Training*, organizations improve the probability of learning success while keeping risks low.

ITIL Project Management and Training

We align all technology training (including cybersecurity) with the ITIL (Information Technology Infrastructure Library) framework to improve the probability of project success. Providing new training is often a requirement of technology projects, and the training team is invited to participate in the new project in the project initiation phase. Since ITIL represents best practices for technology implementation, use, and optimization in *Cybersecurity Training*, we align the ADDIE Model of Instructional Design with the natural cadence of ITIL technology project management (seen later in Figure II.3).

Technology training (Figure II.1) may include hardware (including infrastructure), software, and cybersecurity training (general security literacy, awareness, and specialized role-based training). Hardware training is like software training in that instructional designers can use the same processes and tools to analyze, design, develop, implement, and evaluate hardware training as described in *Cybersecurity Training*. Given the rise in IoT, AI, robotics, and metaverse technologies and devices, organizations are exploring and, where appropriate, developing capabilities, resulting

| Hardware | Input Devices | Output Devices |
| | Processing Devices | Storage Devices |

Software	Cybersecurity Applications	
	Back-End Applications	
	Front-End Applications	

| Awareness Training | General Literacy | |
| | Cybersecurity Awareness | |

Specialized Training	Privileged-Users	Third-Party Stakeholders
	Physical and	Leadership, etc.
	Cybersecurity Personnel	

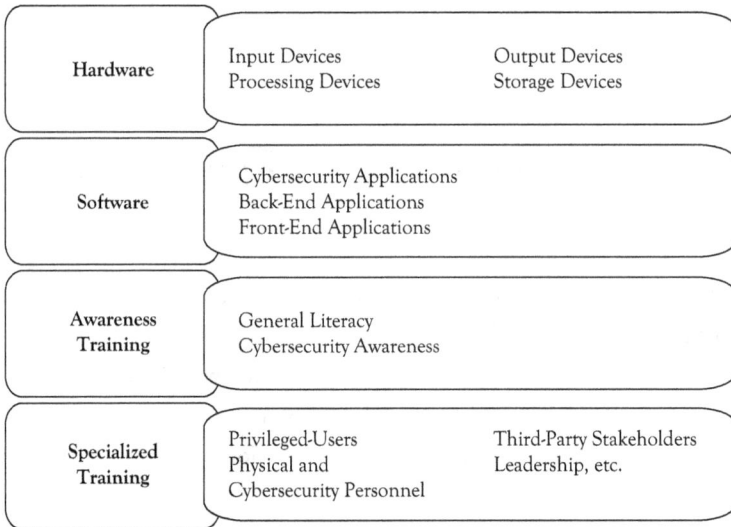

Figure II.1 Technology training categories

in more technology (hardware and software) projects with cybersecurity training implications.

Our focus in *Cybersecurity Training* is on awareness and specialized cybersecurity training; however, those providing hardware and software training (e.g., quantum technologies) can also use the techniques in this book.

Software Training Continuum

Software training can vary on a continuum from open functionality to use case training (Figure II.2). Open functionality training is when the training focus is on using the functions of the software. For example, the learner might receive training in the functions of productivity software like a spreadsheet or project scheduling application. Or a learning management system (LMS) is implemented with basic functionality (e.g., LMS tools and interfaces to other systems) that instructional designers can build and use to provide training. Similarly, a surgeon could receive training in using a robot to assist with surgery. The surgeon would learn about the robotic software, surgical instruments, stapler, sealer, and

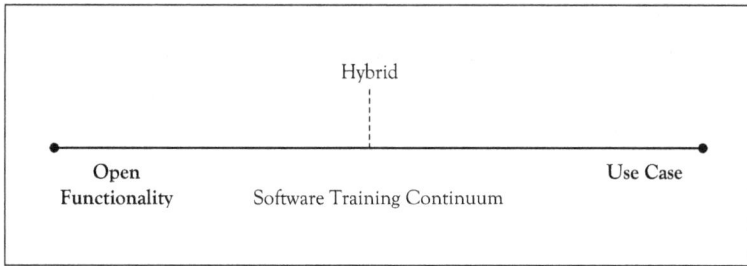

Figure II.2 Software training continuum

cameras/lights. In each of these examples, the learner was taught the basic functions of the software and hardware devices. The user is responsible for applying the learning to achieve the desired result.

At the other end of the training continuum is use case-based training. Use cases are ways the user interacts with the software to accomplish a task or provide a service (Figure II.2). For example, a human resource application may have generic use cases like applying for and approving annual leave. A customer relationship management system may have user-configurable workflows for customer support, marketing, and purchasing; users are trained to follow the processes configured in their new software.

A hybrid application is possible: basic functionality is provided, and the end user can assemble or build components to achieve the desired result; however, there may also be use cases for routine actions. For example, a financial system has both use cases (e.g., end-of-month processes) the finance team routinely completes and open functionality the finance team can use to complete more specialized tasks (e.g., software functionality to trace and investigate suspicious activities).

Therefore, training projects can vary and depend upon the impact and severity of not learning, ranging from simple ADDIE Model templates to formal and large-scale training programs. Organizations can expect more training projects, including:

- *Software application projects*: Software training will vary according to the software training continuum (Figure II.2) from basic functionality to business workflows (use case training). Use case training is more complex as the workflow is only approved at the tail-end of the project during the testing phase (we will look at user acceptance testing later). Therefore, due to delays in user acceptance approval, there is a risk that workflow-based training may be late, resulting in a delayed project go-live. Applications usually do not go-live if the end users are not sufficiently trained.

- *Artificial intelligence projects*: More training will be required as more artificial intelligence (AI) is implemented into the workplace (later upgraded with quantum technologies). Training will cover using a collection of AI technologies and processes to create, protect, implement, and optimize problem-solving and decision making.
- *Automation, programming, and robotic care*: Organizations will provide new learning opportunities related to automation planning, programming (e.g., Python and Qiskit), and robot maintenance as robots and robotics become more common.
- *Hardware*: As more IoT devices are embedded in work, training demand will increase. Hardware-intensive applications like robotics used in surgery will require continual upskilling.
- *Quantum computing applications*: Society is on the cusp of introducing quantum computing into technical ecosystems. Training will incorporate these quantum technologies with significant implications for general awareness and specialized training.
- *NIST awareness and specialized training*: Planning, implementing, and optimizing training that aligns with the NIST Cybersecurity Framework is our focus in *Cybersecurity Training* and expanded in PART II.

Our project management approach to implementing the ADDIE Model of Instructional Design with Bloom's Taxonomy and the Kirkpatrick Model Evaluation, combined with ITIL, ISO risk, and quality management, applies to the other types of training (e.g., manufacturing with collaborative robots) and other cybersecurity standards (Payment Card Industry Data Security Standard—PCI DSS).

Microlearning

Digital technology training ranges between functionality and use case training, requiring varied training techniques and support:

- Search for software training risks and issues;
- Find software training best practices;
- Learn about digital twins and training.

A Project-Oriented Approach to Cybersecurity Training

Not all cybersecurity or technology projects require training. However, when training is required, one can benefit from structured approaches to training (e.g., ADDIE Instructional Design and Bloom's Taxonomy) and learning assessment (Kirkpatrick Model). We align these training approaches with the cadence of the ITIL Service Value Chain and Service Value System (Figure I.5). Organizations can improve the probability of cybersecurity training success by following project management best practices beginning with the project initiation phase.

Initiate the Cybersecurity Project

Recall that it is a best practice (PMBOK® Guide and ITIL) to formally initiate a cybersecurity or technology project through a project approval process. Once the project manager has the approval to proceed with the project, they create a project charter[14] in the initiation phase. The project charter includes the scope (*what*), rationale (*why*), stakeholders overview (*who*), a description of the approach to achieve the desired outcome (*how*), a preliminary high-level budget (*how* much), and schedule (*when*). The top risks and issues may also be included. The project charter is often the first formal opportunity to discuss training at a high level: "is training required?" A severe risk is that a cybersecurity project is initiated, and the training team may be notified late in the project of a training requirement, resulting in a last-minute scramble to provide training. However, you are

---

[14] We create a one-page project charter infographic to orient our teams.

more likely to deliver successful training using the risk-based approach outlined in *Cybersecurity Training*.

ADDIE Model Alignment With Project Management

The ADDIE Model of Instructional Design aligns with project management practices resulting in a natural fit between the two approaches; indeed, the training life cycle mirrors the project life cycle. Both training and project management begin with a demand, progress through a development and implementation process, and benefit from multiple assessment points should corrective changes be required. Both instructional design and project management approaches progressively elaborate the design and delivery of the end product or service. Both training best practices and project management delivery approaches allow for tailoring and combining and are specially enhanced with stakeholder engagement. Both training and project management involve continual improvement.

Van Rooij (2010) reviewed 11 instructional design models and concluded that:

(1) a formal, documented process of project management is essential to the success of any instructional design project, (2) those who manage instructional design projects must be skilled project managers as well as skilled instructional designers, and (3) project management is embedded in the successful execution of the various phases and stages of the instructional design process.

Therefore, applying a project management approach to the ADDIE Model of Instructional Design aligns naturally and can improve the probability of a successful learning project. At the heart of instructional design is quality management (Brown and Green 2016): The value proposition is if you follow the ADDIE Model of Instructional Design process, you will improve the probability of successful teaching and learning while minimizing risks. ADDIE aligns with ISO quality management principles, such as a focus on quality assurance and continual improvement.

While the training team may be notified in the initiation phase that a project has been approved with training implications, the collaborative work begins in earnest in the project plan phase (Figure II.3).

The heart of *Cybersecurity Training* is illustrated in Figure II.3: aligning the ADDIE Model of Instructional Design with cybersecurity project management.[15] We often refer to Figure II.3 and the concept of project-oriented instructional design throughout *Cybersecurity Training*.

Project Plan Phase

The goal of the planning phase is to develop and approve a project plan the team will follow through the project phases. The project plan may vary from a comprehensive (Figure II.4) to a concise plan of a few pages for a smaller initiative. Again, we recommend the "Goldilocks Approach": not too much, not too little, just the right amount of project management to deliver projects successfully.

Organizations provide teams with lean project plans with just enough content to guide and deliver the sponsor's project requirements. The training manager may initiate and plan training while the project manager initiates and plans the cybersecurity project (Figure II.3).

Scope management: The project plan will include the project scope and describes "what" will be delivered. The project manager may create a work breakdown structure (WBS) and a requirements traceability matrix to document and track the project scope. We recommend including a high-level WBS since it illustrates the scope that visually oriented stakeholders appreciate. The requirements traceability matrix allows the project team to track scope completion through the project life cycle (more fully illustrated later in Table II.2) and reduces the probability of scope creep. Training can also be tracked to completion with the requirements traceability matrix. However, the level of training detail will be more granular

---

[15] We do not include the initiation phase in Figure II.3 because there is usually little training involvement other than the project manager notifying the training manager that a new project is initiated, and the training team will be invited to future planning and project activities. The training manager will appreciate receiving the project charter to better understand the project.

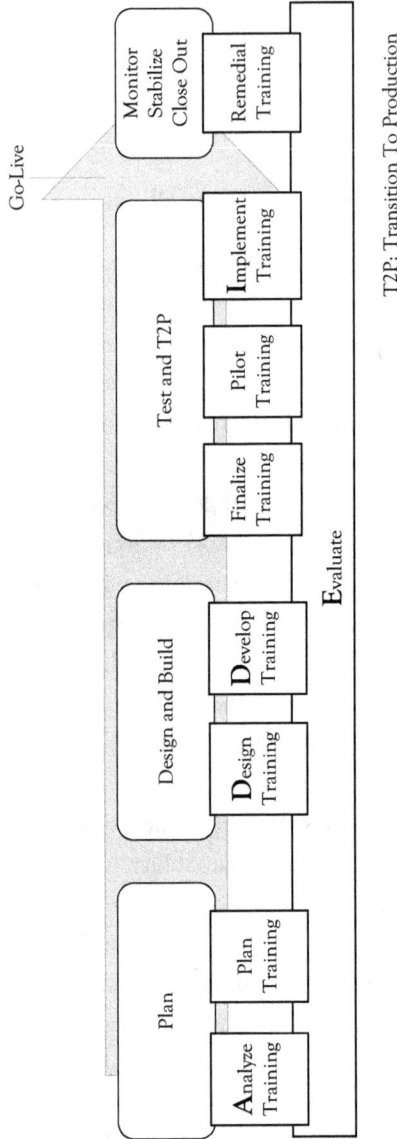

Figure II.3 ADDIE Model aligned with project management

Project Plan									
Scope	Schedule	Cost	Risk	Quality	Procurement	Resources	Stakeholders	Communications	Integration
Design-in Training and Learning (and Security!) into the Project Plan									

Figure II.4 Project plan contents

in the training documents than in the sponsor's project plan. The training team can get an overall sense of project progress by reviewing the requirements traceability matrix throughout the project.

Schedule management: The schedule may be a high-level Gantt chart (e.g., commonly called a "bar chart") or a detailed network diagram (e.g., critical path network) and outlines when work starts and is completed. Task dependencies and who completes the work can also be planned and monitored with scheduling software. However, a perennial issue organizations face in technology projects is the large number of projects delivered late (you might search online to find out the project success rate for your industry). Therefore, there is a high probability the training team may be presented with project schedules likely to change. Projects are often late because single-point duration estimates (e.g., "testing will take *12 days*") are used to develop schedules. Single-point estimates are deficient because they do not easily account for risk and are subject to "padding" (e.g., 10 percent contingency is added to the schedule).

Instead of single-point duration estimates, we use and recommend a range of estimates based on PERT (program evaluation and review technique) that considers project risks resulting in better duration estimates. We estimate under three project conditions (e.g., three scenarios): "perfect" conditions, "likely" conditions, and "outrageous" conditions (PLOs). When PLO estimates account for risks, project managers develop improved schedules. Estimating with PLOs takes less time because estimating is easier with PLO estimates. Estimating is performed for three different project conditions: (1) perfect, where everything goes better than planned; (2) a likely scenario where the project team faces some issues but also experiences some luck; and (3) outrageous where everything seems to go wrong resulting in compound risks and issues. Single-point estimates force the subject matter expert (SME) to provide one number to represent all possible scenarios that confound the estimate provider! Thus, estimates are captured for three different conditions[16] rather than to represent all the different scenarios with single-point estimates—a challenging task. The project schedule from the planning phase is an input to training and is integrated into the ADDIE training project life cycle (Figure II.3).

Cost management: Some technology projects do not require cost management since they are internal projects. However, when a budget is required, there are standard cost management processes to follow. Budget-related risks and issues are common in projects, including training projects. A common risk is due to project cost overruns, there is a risk that the project training may be reduced, resulting in a training scope reduction. Again, an online search for overbudget technology projects in your industry can help you gauge the degree of risk to your projects. We use and recommend three-point estimates (e.g., PLO's) to improve the quality of budgets and the probability of completing technology and training projects on budget.

Procurement management: The process of acquiring external goods and services for the project. The training project manager may onboard external content developers, trainers, and other specialists through the project procurement process. Procurement is an early project activity, and the training team may be asked for procurement-related requirements. The requirements traceability matrix tracks contracted deliverables (e.g., training resources) through the procurement life cycle and project closeout.

Resources management: Project resource management involves assigning people and equipment to project tasks per the scope, budget, and schedule. These resources may be internal or external and are traditionally illustrated with an organizational chart (Figure II.5). Therefore, we recommend the training project manager represent the training function

---

[16] You can learn more about range estimates in *Shields Up: Cybersecurity Project Management.*

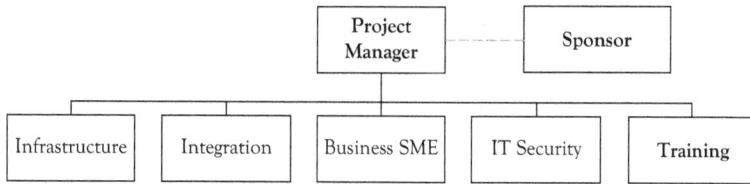

Figure II.5 Project organizational chart

early in the project (e.g., initiation phase) to ensure successful training and learning.

Traditionally, the project is led by a project manager with direction from the project sponsor. The training team will collaborate primarily with the project manager, sponsor, and the sponsor's representative (e.g., business SME). The business subject matter expert (e.g., finance department) represents the requirements and use cases for the project (e.g., complete month-end reconciliation). The business SME will also bring into the design best practices represented in their discipline-specific frameworks (e.g., Generally Accepted Accounting Principles for a finance project) and standards (ISO 20022 Electronic Data Interchange for a finance project). The project manager works with the IT security team to protect the new application and with other IT teams, such as cloud services and integration. The SME will be IT security when the project upgrades IT security software (e.g., new detection capabilities).

Somewhere in the IT department will be a release manager or someone with that role. This critical role ensures that the new product or service is implemented while keeping risks low and quality high. There is an ITIL Release and Deployment Management practice that provides best practices. The project manager plans with the release manager, then later in the project, coordinates the go-live following ITIL release management best practices[17]: "The project manager brings project management;

---

[17] In *Shields Up*, we explain how we created and used a T2P template of 32 activities to transition the new service safely and securely into the production phase. Indeed, we identified the early start for each T2P activity and were able to complete 60 percent of the activities before the T2P phase. Bringing forward the right work improves the probability of project success and celebratory lunches at the end of the project!

the sponsor brings discipline-specific best practices and requirements." In *Cybersecurity Training*, when we refer to the "project manager," we mean the overall project manager, as seen in Figure II.5. Training can be considered a work package or subproject of the main project led by a training project manager, training manager, or training lead; we use these three training leadership roles interchangeably.

Stakeholder management: Stakeholders are those interested in the product or service delivered by the project. They can influence (Figure II.6A) or are influenced by the project because they use the product or the service delivered through the project (Figure II.6B). There is a risk in projects that not all the stakeholders are identified early enough. The project manager may be unaware of some stakeholders influencing the project (e.g., the governance board or the chief of manufacturing operations). Or some of the end users are not fully represented, resulting in functionality or use case gaps or poorly designed workflows, for example. Therefore, the risk of omitting stakeholders can lead to failed projects. The training team can complete a stakeholder analysis (e.g., Figure II.6) to better understand training stakeholders. For large audiences, it may be helpful to adopt a persona approach, inferring characteristics not of one discreet individual but of a group of stakeholders, such as learners. Using empathy mapping and personas, techniques from design thinking, the instructional designer can approximate the needs of most learners in each learner persona, later validating hypotheses with members of the learner persona we seek to empathize with or understand. We also recommend that where appropriate, training leadership takes the role of influencer (Figure II.6A) to improve the probability that training requirements are delivered.

Are there other stakeholder management tools and techniques? The literature provides stakeholder management "guidance" by prescribing tools like expert judgment, data gathering and analysis, decision making, and meetings. We use and recommend the "three-questions" technique (Skulmoski and Hartman 2000) and complete a Done-Won-Who exercise. When is the project done? What must be delivered for the project to be considered wildly successful (won)? Who gets to vote on the first two questions? By asking these three questions, project managers better understand their project (training and otherwise) and stakeholders.

A

Stakeholders ═══ Influence ═══▶ Project

Internal
- Sponsor
- Leadership
- Technical Leadership
- Board

B

Project ═══ Influences ═══▶ Stakeholders

End users of the product
or service delivered by the
project team

External
- Regulators
- Government
- Contractor Leadership
- Society

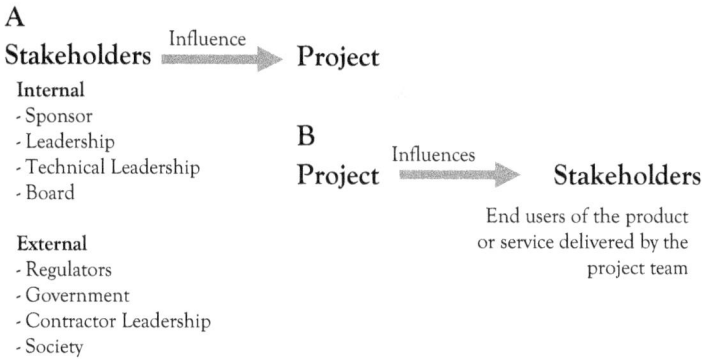

Figure II.6 Stakeholder influence

Communications management: The organization and control of project information so the right information is available to the right stakeholders at the right time. When the project includes training, end users are notified of training. However, scheduling, notifying, registering, and delivering training have many inherent risks; therefore, we advise the training team to contribute to communications planning for the overall project.

Quality management: Quality management is often poorly done on technology projects; if the project is late, over budget, or dissatisfies some stakeholders, there are quality management issues. Our approach to quality management is to build-in quality (and security). We focus on quality assurance: templates, processes, tools, and training to guide subsequent work. We do not use project management tools that repeatedly fail (e.g., single-point estimates). The goal is a lean and adaptive approach to technology project management.

Risk management: All projects, especially technology projects, face risks and issues. Therefore, one of the most important tasks a project manager and the project team can do is to manage risks and issues. Prudent project managers include risk and issue management as a standing agenda item in weekly status meetings and regularly use a simple risk register to monitor and control risks and issues. Our risk treatment/response focuses on risk prevention. When we ask, "how are you?" we want to know how our team member is doing, but we are also looking for risk clues. Therefore, when the team member responds, "busy," we ask, "What's keeping you busy?"

"Any late nights lately? How was your weekend?" to better understand the risks and issues facing our teams. Our goal is to create a risk-aware project culture where our entire team (internal and external) adopts proactive risk management best practices.

Integration management: The project manager brings together all the elements of the project plan in project integration management (Figure II.4). After the project is approved, the project manager monitors the project plan throughout the project. The project manager adapts and adjusts to keep the project plan integrated and on track. However, sometimes significant changes are required to deliver the project, and the project manager successfully follows the change management process (also known as change control).

In *Cybersecurity Training*, we align with the best practices outlined in the PMBOK® Guide and ITIL technology management best practices (e.g., technology testing and release management), where both encourage the user to tailor their approaches (PMBOK® Guide and ITIL) to the reader's projects. We design-in cybersecurity best practices (e.g., secure by design) by combining and tailoring NIST Cybersecurity Framework best practices. Finally, we design-in training best practices detailed in the ADDIE Model of Instructional Design, Bloom's Taxonomy, and the Kirkpatrick Model of Evaluation into the project plan (Figure II.7).

Thus, we combine training best practices into the training project plan for the reader. The training team can provide more effective training if they apply project management tools and processes and understand where they fit into the overall project plan.

A common approach to developing the project plan is for the project manager to meet individually and iteratively with critical stakeholders. The project manager will meet separately with members from IT security, IT infrastructure, IT integration, business units, and so on. The project manager will meet with key stakeholders to validate the scope and add more detail to the budget, schedule, risks, and so on (Figure II.7). The project manager and core team will develop a high-level project plan (Figure II.4) and present it to the stakeholders at a project planning workshop.

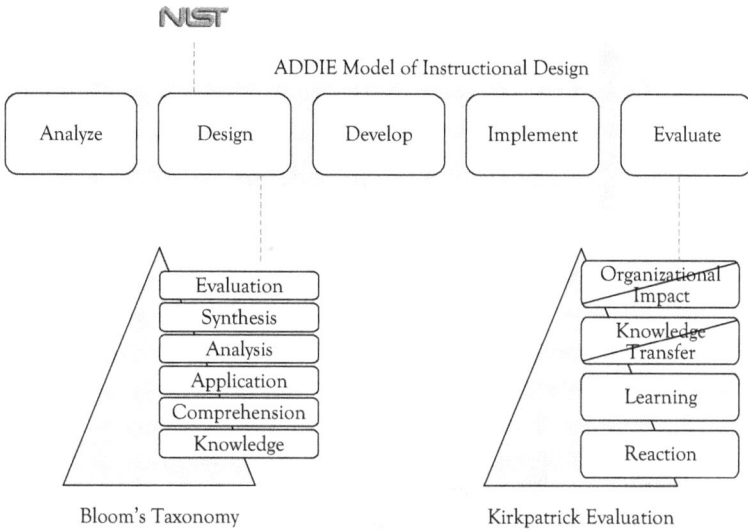

Figure II.7 Model alignment—ADDIE, Bloom's Taxonomy, and Kirkpatrick Evaluation

Project Planning Workshop

The project planning workshop is a critical milestone as it brings together key stakeholders to endorse the scope and elaborate other project plan elements like the schedule. Often, the feedback is iterative, where the sponsor's expectations are better understood, and project participants can share any concerns. The result is the project stakeholders "endorse" the project plan, followed by the project manager seeking approval from the project change control board to proceed to the next phase—project design.

The training team will better understand the training requirements, schedule, budget, and key risks and issues when they attend the project planning workshop. Training risks and issues can be raised at this workshop and help to set expectations since the project sponsor will be in attendance. The sponsor needs to hear that there is a possibility the project can fail. Still, with their assistance, the probability of success improves (e.g., the project manager requests the project sponsor provide on-time feedback and approvals to keep the project on schedule).

Microlearning

Organizing workshops to collaborate is widely used in projects with plentiful online resources:

- Search for project planning workshop activities and agenda.
- Look for how to facilitate workshops, including design thinking workshops.
- Search for "persona," "empathy map," and "sponsor user."

ADDIE: *Plan Training and Learning*

Planning is a training project critical success factor; even though the training team may wish to start developing content, they will benefit from approaching training as a project and developing a training project plan. The instructional designer creates a project plan to satisfy the training requirements. The amount of planning depends upon the impact of not learning; the instructional designer develops less formal and comprehensive training plans for less impactful training. As the impact of not learning increases, the instructional designer creates a more comprehensive training project plan.[18] The training project plan usually includes:

- *Training scope*: The scope statement describes "what" the training project includes. For example, "develop an online NIST-aligned cybersecurity awareness module for board members by the end of June." Often, the scope is elaborated in a WBS (e.g., the hierarchy of work).
- *Training rationale*: The rationale statement describes "why" the training is required. For example, "the last internal phishing campaign revealed significant gaps in employees' safe cybersecurity practices, resulting in the goal to improve cybersecurity awareness through additional training."

---

[18] For more information and guidance to create a project plan, the reader is advised to review *Shields Up: Cybersecurity Project Management*, where the reader is taken through the project planning and implementation process that is applicable to training project plans.

- *Training stakeholders*: Identify the critical stakeholders for your training, such as the project manager, project sponsor, learners, training project team, content SMEs, and trainers.
- *Training budget*: Some training projects do not require a budget, as only internal resources are used. However, resource utilization may be tracked through full-time equivalents (FTEs) or another approach to effort measurement. Should external resources be required (e.g., trainers, third-party-provided content, etc.), then a "bottom-up" budget can be developed based on the scope of work represented in the WBS. If required, project managers often work with the finance department to plan and map project expense reporting to the organization's correct chart of accounts.
- *Training schedule*: Instructional designers use the WBS as an input to create a Gantt chart (bar chart schedule) for the training project. A more detailed project schedule (network diagram) can be developed once the high-level Gantt chart is endorsed. The training schedule should align with the approved project plan and reflect the ADDIE design process (Figure II.3). We favor PLO estimates for task durations and budget estimates since they account for risk. A confounding schedule-related issue in technology projects is the IT SME's priority in operations; operations-oriented SMEs usually prioritize resolving high-priority tickets over project activities. Therefore, project schedules can be a bit unpredictable for technology training projects.
- *Training risks*: Risk management is a critical success factor in projects. The fundamental principle is to prevent risks from becoming issues with negative impacts on projects. Cybersecurity, in essence, is risk management. Therefore, the project manager and IT security team are risk-aware. You are a valued team member with a risk-aware mindset. The only reason training projects fail is that risks have become issues negatively impacting the project.

- *Training communications*: The training project manager will communicate extensively with the stakeholders and the project manager. Project communications often include information about training, and the training project manager is encouraged to collaborate in project communications planning.
- *Training procurement*: The process of acquiring new goods (e.g., training content, simulations, and assessment instruments) and services (e.g., trainers from the software vendor). A tendering process may be required to purchase outside training materials and services, requiring procurement lead time to be added to the schedule. Training project managers often work with the procurement department to procure goods and services just-in-time.
- *Training human resources*: Managing the training teams (internal and external) to achieve the training project objectives (e.g., time, cost, scope, stakeholder satisfaction, etc.).

You will notice that our training project plan categories align with the overall project plan, allowing easy integration and risk reduction (Figure II.3).

Instructional designers follow a project-oriented approach to training and identify in and out of scope items. It is the learner's responsibility to apply what was learned and for the training sponsor and business line manager to evaluate the transfer of learning and performance. However, there are things the training team can do with the training sponsor to improve the probability of successful learning transfer:

- *Managerial support*: A servant leader manager supports continual and self-directed learning that allows and helps the learner to transfer new competencies. This *superstar* manager provides helpful feedback and support. The manager sets up the environmental conditions for success. For example, a simple reward system for successfully applying learning, job design involvement, or leadership encouragement helps some learners apply what they have learned. Alternatively, the absence of leadership support for training and learning might be further investigated as a training risk. Ed Deming wrote about managerial responsibilities: "Leadership is *only* 99% of the problem." Servant leaders play a significant role in the successful transfer of learning. The training team may suggest the training sponsor create a simple transfer of learning plan (e.g., one-page) to organize their thoughts. After all, no manager wants one of their direct reports to cause a cybersecurity incident despite completing general awareness training. Research shows the sooner the knowledge transfer occurs (e.g., within the first week or month), the greater the probability of success.

- *Goal setting*: Many learners improve the probability of successful learning transfer when they set goals and develop a simple plan (including scheduled time to refresh learning). One might include a goal-setting exercise during the cybersecurity class to improve the probability of the transfer of learning. Training goals and outcomes can be linked to annual employee performance assessments for critical role-based learning.

The critical success factors and best practices related to project planning also apply to training projects and are outlined in this book.

ADDIE: *Training Analysis*

Instructional designers begin their training analysis by understanding the desired change(s) in the learner(s) they wish to achieve. They analyze the training requirements for the needs, tasks, and learners (Figure II.8). While their planning and analysis began in the project planning phase, the instructional designer continues analysis into the project design phase by adding more detail to their plans and training assets. Some organizations keep a prioritized backlog of training

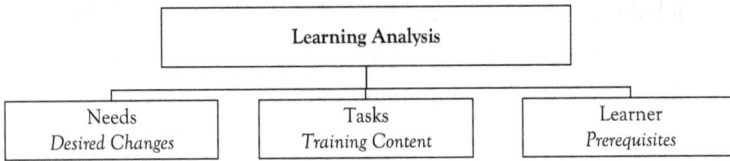

Figure II.8 Learning analysis categories

requests that can be reviewed when new content is being developed. The backlog of training requests works similarly to the product backlog in agile project management.

Learning Needs Analysis

The instructional designer conducts learning needs analysis and focuses on the desired changes regarding skills, attitudes, and knowledge. The instructional designer considers the importance of attitude in effective cybersecurity behaviors when conducting the needs analysis. Cybersecurity training programs can include content that shapes and reinforces the organization's cybersecurity culture (e.g., cybersecurity is everyone's responsibility). The needs analysis begins by examining the training request:

1. What changes are desired (e.g., improved CSIRT team capabilities to detect, respond, and recover capabilities from cybersecurity incidents)?
2. Who has requested the change (e.g., Chief Information Security Officer)?
3. Where will the change occur (e.g., IT and business partners)?
4. Are other options available besides instruction (e.g., practice without instruction and outsourcing)?

The instructional design discipline is mature and evolving; practitioners are fortunate to benefit from a tradition of evidence-based practice with a broad and deep body of knowledge. For example, Morrison and colleagues (2019) describe needs analysis techniques ranging from lean to comprehensive approaches, including the classic consulting approach: plan the needs analysis, collect data, analyze the data, and submit the final report. Smith and Ragan offer the Discrepancy-Based Needs Assessment Model (Brown and Green 2016):

1. *Identify the instructional goals*: The instructional designer can use the NIST and NICE frameworks to identify their role-based and/or general awareness instructional goals (Figure I.9).
2. *Describe the current situation*: The NIST Cybersecurity Framework audit provides details about the current situation.
3. *List the gap between the current and target state of ability*: The instructional designer identifies the gap between the current and target NIST functional capabilities.
4. *Prioritize the learning requirements*: Sponsors help prioritize the capabilities they wish to improve (e.g., managed with the product backlog in Figure I.20).
5. *Determine how to address the learning requirements*: The instructional designer identifies how to deliver the prioritized capabilities.

For example, a gap may be identified and addressed in general awareness cybersecurity training. The organization wishes to improve its members' understanding and ability to manage sophisticated threats from deep fake videos. The NIST Cybersecurity Framework provides guidance. Updating training content with deep fake content aligns with the Literacy Training and Awareness—Social Engineering and Mining control (NIST SP 800-53, REV 5, AT-3.3, 61).

Completing a training needs analysis determines the formality of training and learning. For example, an analysis may reveal that minor updates to existing training materials are required to satisfy the training requirements of the new project. However, other projects may have new training requirements. The more significant the impact of insufficient learning, the more formal training and learning evaluation can be. While there are other training models, Bloom's Taxonomy and the Kirkpatrick Model of Evaluation are industry standards that are easy to understand, proven, and generally accepted. Bloom's Taxonomy and the Kirkpatrick Model can be used in most training, most of the time including cybersecurity training. Therefore, we combine the ADDIE Model of Instruction Design with Bloom's Taxonomy and the Kirkpatrick Model of Evaluation as fundamental elements in the *Cybersecurity Training* tool kit (Figure II.7).

Gap Analysis

Completing a gap analysis of training/learning needs is central to the needs analysis.[19] Like others, we use the NIST Cybersecurity Framework and related NIST documents about cybersecurity training (Figure I.9) to design cybersecurity training (Figure II.7). The gap analysis problem-solving technique is well respected and broadly used, supported by online resources. The NIST publications also provide detailed gap analysis ("comparison of profiles") and cybersecurity improvement directions (NIST 2003; NIST 2023).

The NIST Cybersecurity Framework approach to training follows a project delivery approach. Begin by defining scope, analyzing stakeholders (e.g., learners), documenting requirements (e.g., learning outcomes), developing, delivering, and evaluating training, and so on. Instructional designers write learning outcomes for general awareness and specialized role-based training. Knowledge and skills are detailed in the NIST role-based training special publication (NIST 2014), with examples following (Table II.1). Instructional designers find detailed guidance in the NIST documentation to write learning outcomes for either NIST general awareness or specialized training based on their gap analysis. The NICE Workforce Framework (NIST 2020b) can be used and is based on the skills and knowledge required to complete tasks. Since there is a better transfer of learning when learners are involved, instructional designers seek content guidance from the IT security team during the design phase to improve relevancy. Therefore, the learning outcomes (at a minimum) focus on advancing cybersecurity knowledge and skills capabilities.

The NIST Cybersecurity Framework also includes guidance for cybersecurity roles (NICCS 2022). In *Cybersecurity Training*, we bring

---

[19] Greg first studied competency gaps as they relate to organizational readiness (or lack of readiness) early in his research career: G. Skulmoski. June 2001. "Project Maturity and Competence Interface," *Cost Engineering* 43, no. 6.

Table II.1 Learning outcomes example

Training type	Learning outcome
General Awareness	Skill: The learner will be able to raise a ticket if they encounter suspicious cyber activity
General Awareness	Knowledge: The learner will understand the basic principles of phishing
Specialized: Systems Security	Knowledge: The learner will understand web services (NIST 2014, WT-1, 70)
Specialized: Systems Security	Skill: The learner will be able to identify forensic footprints (NIST 2014, DF-18, 69)
Specialized: Information Systems Security Leadership	Knowledge: The learner will understand IT/cybersecurity program management and project management principles and techniques (NIST 2014, PM-2, 74)
Specialized: Information Systems Security	Skill: The learner will be able to develop security policies and procedures (NIST 2014, PM-8, 75)

the reader to the NIST Cybersecurity Framework, and they tailor and combine for their unique organization as only they can.

After the needs assessment (Figure II.9), one may find that the intervention required to arrive at the target state may be achieved through non-training means, such as revising a policy, procedure, or business workflow. For example, the organization may require certain third-party contractors to take cybersecurity training, including content about detecting deep fakes within the supply chain. The organization may already have sufficient training content but may wish to extend training to additional supply chain partners. This goal can be accomplished by revising their contracts, policies, and procedures that require third-party partners to complete general awareness and a specialized training module specific to external partners.

The organization also aligns with the NIST Special Publication for Cybersecurity Role-Based Training by delivering content about social engineering and with the NIST Security and Privacy Controls for Information Systems and Organizations (2020a) special publication. When noninstructional requirements are identified during the gap analysis, you may forward the requirement to the suitable business unit for resolution. Thus, the NIST Cybersecurity Framework and special publications guide general awareness and specialized role-based training. Therefore, please

		NIST Cybersecurity Framework
		Provide awareness and specialized cybersecurity training for third-party stakeholders (e.g., contractors, suppliers, etc.) (NIST, 2018, PR-AT-03; NIST, 2023, PR-AT-02)

Needs Analysis	Extend Training	NIST Special Publication for Cybersecurity Role-Based Training
Improve Deep Fake Detection Capabilities	Third-Party Stakeholders	PS-2: Knowledge of and promotion of general awareness regarding the use of social engineering techniques (NIST-SP 800-53, Rev. 5, 2014)

		NIST Security and Privacy Controls for Information Systems and Organizations
		AT-2.3 Literacy Training and Awareness: Social Engineering and Mining (NIST-SP 800-53, Rev. 5, 2020a)

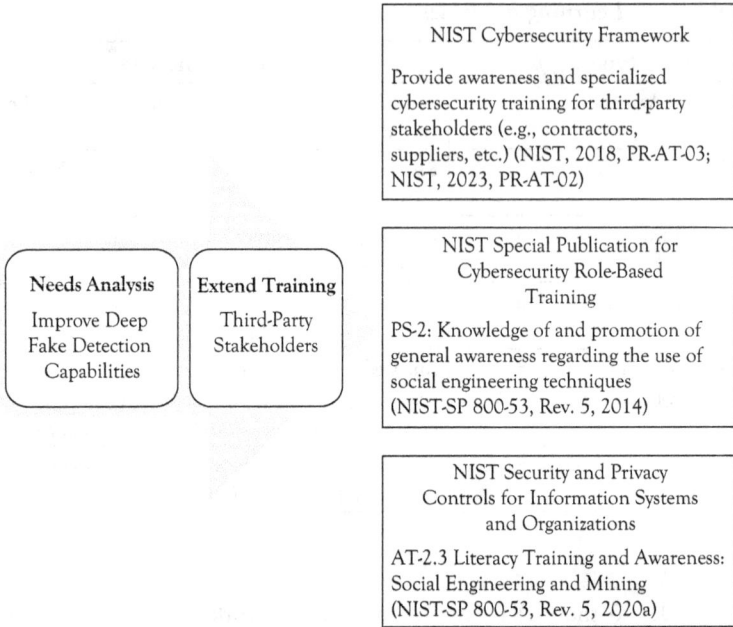

Figure II.9 Training needs analysis and NIST alignment

spend some time with the recommended NIST publications to discover their applicability as you read this book.

Another way to look at needs analysis is to ask three questions (Skulmoski and Hartman 2000): When is the training done? What learning should occur for the training to be considered wildly successful? And who gets to vote on the first two questions? Unsuccessful training is sometimes due to not identifying the critical stakeholders and focusing solely on the training requestor. The trainer may advise: "Don't design and develop what we cannot deliver." When one asks the "three questions" in training and projects in general, alignment and project success are more likely. When one asks the three questions after a formal needs analysis, one better articulates the needs analysis, especially when the criticality of learning is high. The three questions are a project stakeholder analysis technique.

Learning Task Analysis

The needs analysis informs the instructional designer whether training is required and if an element in the learning ecosystem can be improved (e.g., a policy and procedure). They also identify the training sponsor and detail the learning environment (e.g., online training module delivered through the organization's LMS) in the needs assessment. The instructional designer conducts a task analysis during or after the needs analysis. Task analysis details the training content (skills and knowledge). Indeed, task analysis is often the most critical aspect of the instructional design process. Cybersecurity training content (skills and knowledge) is documented in the *NIST Special Publication: A Role-Based Model for Federal Information Technology/Cybersecurity Training* (NIST 2014). The training sponsor and training team can review and prioritize the knowledge and skills using the NIST special publication for role-based training as part of their task analysis.

Learner Analysis

Learner analysis (Figure II.8) includes determining the learner's prerequisite knowledge and skills (competencies). Learner analysis is simplified by using the NIST role-based training categories (e.g., privileged users) as they are common roles to most organizations (NIST 2018, 31):

1. *Privileged users*: An SME authorized to perform security-relevant functions that ordinary users are not authorized to conduct.
2. *Service desk, physical, and other cybersecurity personnel*: IT and physical security personnel benefit from supplementary cybersecurity role-based training.
3. *Third-party stakeholders*: External partners like service providers, vendors, supply-side partners, demand-side partners, alliances, consortiums, and investors. The relationship may be contractual or noncontractual. Increasingly, third-party stakeholders are valued cybersecurity partners as organizations strive to strengthen their entire technology ecosystem.
4. *Senior leadership*: Cybersecurity role-based training is required for senior leadership as they have unique responsibilities regarding cybersecurity readiness.

For example, the organization may complete its analysis and conclude that it needs to develop specialized training for seven positions

```
                                    ┌──────────────────────────────────────┐
                                    │         1. Privileged Users          │
                                    └──────────────────────────────────────┘
                                    ┌──────────────────────────────────────┐
                                    │          2. Service Desk             │
                                    └──────────────────────────────────────┘
                                    ┌──────────────────────────────────────┐
                                    │    3. Physical (Security Guards)     │
                                    └──────────────────────────────────────┘
┌──────────────────────────┐        ┌──────────────────────────────────────┐
│           NIST           │        │        4. IT SME–General             │
│ Specialized Role-Based   │────────│                                      │
│        Training          │        └──────────────────────────────────────┘
└──────────────────────────┘        ┌──────────────────────────────────────┐
                                    │        5. IT SME–Security            │
                                    └──────────────────────────────────────┘
                                    ┌──────────────────────────────────────┐
                                    │          6. Third-Party              │
                                    └──────────────────────────────────────┘
                                    ┌──────────────────────────────────────┐
                                    │          7. Leadership               │
                                    └──────────────────────────────────────┘
```

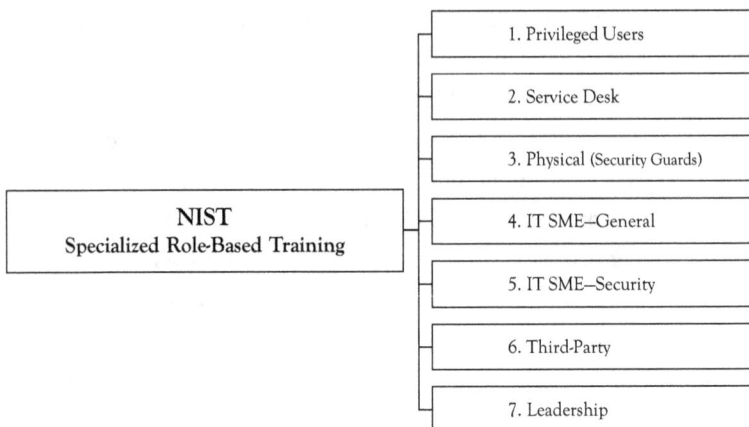

Figure II.10 Seven roles/positions identified example

(Figure II.10). The reader can refer to the *Á Role-Based Model for Federal Information Technology/Cybersecurity Training* (NIST 2014) for recommended skills and knowledge for their prioritized roles. Depending upon your unique training requirements, the reader may begin with fewer or expand beyond seven roles.

The organization may develop modularized content (the "Box Car Approach"[20] that can be used sequentially as the learner progresses, Figure II.11). For example, Module 1 might be required for all privileged and technical users (Figure II.10). The intermediate training (Modules 1 and 2) is required for all IT-General and IT-Security personnel. Only the IT-Security personnel take Module 3 as part of their advanced training.

Related to the Box Car approach, one can also improve the design with scaffolding: content is broken into smaller units, and the learner progresses from easy to more challenging concepts. The trainer can also provide support to help the students achieve higher learning. For example, the trainer can explain a cybersecurity concept in multiple ways, supported by illustrations to ensure learner understanding. Or the learner might be given the "perfect" solution to help guide their design.

---

[20] We attribute the innovative Box Car approach to curriculum design to Marc Chiu, where it was used to design, develop, and implement training for 3,500 caregivers on core systems required to safely open Cleveland Clinic Abu Dhabi and provide world class healthcare. The Box Car approach works!

Advanced	Module 1	Module 2	Module 3
Intermediate	Module 1	Module 2	
Introduction	Module 1		

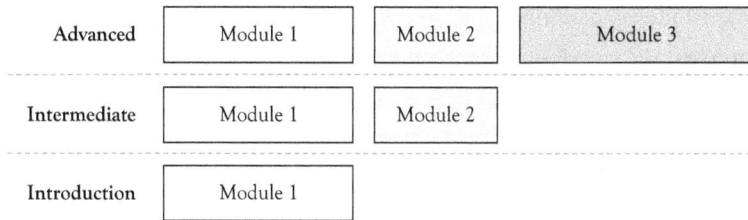

Figure II.11 "Box Car" content design

Scaffolding is breaking down learning objectives into smaller components that are easier for the learner to complete, and the instructor is available to provide support until the learner can complete the activity independently.

After completing a thorough ADDIE-based analysis of training and learning, sometimes the approved project plan may need to change. For example, the learner analysis may conclude by recommending more training than initially approved. Therefore, more time will be needed for content design, development, pilot testing, and delivery. As a result, the approved project schedule may be extended through the project change control process.

Learning analysis (needs, tasks, and learner, Figure II.8) improves the probability of a coherent training program.

Microlearning

Instructional designers have a long history of analysis with a vast body of knowledge online:

- Look for how to conduct a learning needs analysis.
- Find or generate training needs analysis templates.
- Identify key learning needs analysis risks.
- Find related infographics, such as the learning needs analysis process.

Project Design Phase

The design phase embodies *what* is required and *how* to deliver it. Designing is a collaborative and social process enhanced when the intended users are involved (e.g., learners and instructors). The design phase follows planning and analysis, and the goal is to develop an approved suite of design artifacts (e.g., a low-level infrastructure design, integration design, and application detailed design) that the build team can use for a software-based project. When IT training is required (e.g., IT Service Desk, end users, etc.), training design begins in the project design phase (Figure II.3).

The training project manager's goal is to achieve a "shared understanding" of the training deliverables; the stakeholders have the same understanding of training success. For example, the instructional designer wants to avoid the issue that training is about to be delivered, and the trainer asks for a facilitator guide when none has been developed. When one identifies and documents the training deliverables, they are more likely to avoid an incomplete set of training artifacts. We set up and recommend a training deliverable traceability matrix (Table II.2).

Table II.2 ADDIE Model aligned awareness training traceability matrix

Training topic	Analyze	Design	Develop	Implement	Evaluate
Physical security	✓				
Cybersecurity	✓				
Passwords/authentication	✓	✓			
Internet and e-mails	✓				
~~Removable Media~~	✓	Removed from scope (change request #228)			
Social media	✓				
Cloud security	✓				
Mobile devices	✓				
Working remotely	✓				
Public WiFi	✓				
Working from home	✓				
Phishing	✓	✓			
Social engineering	✓				
Ransomware	✓	✓			
Data privacy	✓				
Cyber incident response	✓				

We use the ADDIE Model traceability matrix to track requirements completion, and it operates like a Kanban board. The project manager may also use a requirements traceability matrix to track project requirements, including training, through to completion. The requirements traceability matrix improves transparency and quality and reduces project risks for the training team.

Design teams often include specialists like graphic artists, content creators, project managers, programmers, evaluation gurus, and others that must be coordinated during the design activities. It is often a balancing act between too much and too little involvement of the design team in design workshops since they likely manage competing demands for their time and expertise (e.g., they may work on multiple projects). Again, we follow the "Goldilocks Approach": not too much, not too little, just the right amount of project management to deliver the product or service successfully.

Design Workshop

A common approach to developing an information system design is to complete a series of design workshops to capture user requirements, map out processes, identify printing and reporting requirements, and so on. For more impactful and critical projects, the Delphi method to obtain requirements or design consensus can be used (Skulmoski et al. 2007). Stakeholders (e.g., subject matter experts and end users) attend design workshops hosted by the project management team. They follow an incremental and iterative approach to develop and refine the project requirements and design. The project management team develops the design documents, including an overview of training. Once the design documents are approved, the instructional design team can design and develop the new learning experience. However, some design work can proceed before ALL design document approval; fast-tracking is a project management technique where one overlaps two project phases. While fast-tracking has the appealing possibility of condensing the schedule, there are also risks of proceeding before precedent work is completed and approved.

ADDIE: Design Training and Learning

The ADDIE Design phase uses a structured approach to map the end-to-end learner experience. The instructional designer brings into the ADDIE Design phase their analysis from the previous ADDIE Analysis phase (Figure II.8). They specify learning outcomes, the learning experience, content, tools, structure, evaluation strategy and tactics, logistics and resources, learner registration process, and so on in a concise design strategy. The ADDIE Design document is collaboratively developed and approved by the training sponsor. The ADDIE Design document may also include deliverables that, upon completion and acceptance, the ADDIE Design phase ends, and the ADDIE Develop phase begins. However, developing and approving training materials can occur throughout the project life cycle (Figure II.3) rather than neatly into ADDIE phases due to the nature of technology training. Only after user acceptance testing (UAT) is completed and the training requirements fully approved can we confidently complete training materials development (discussed later in systems testing, Figure II.23).

A concise ADDIE Design document may include the following:

1. Project overview and rationale: a manufacturing system upgrade with manufacturing and cybersecurity training.
2. Training goals and objectives: relate to the NIST Cybersecurity Framework where appropriate.
3. Training subjects and learning outcomes: a table format.
4. Evaluation strategy: reactive, formative, summative, and lessons learned and tactics (e.g., multiple-choice questions with a leaderboard to track progress).
5. Logistics: registration, resources, trainers, training rooms, LMS, and so on.
6. Other: a third-party simulation will be purchased and used.
7. Appendixes: training requirements traceability matrix.

Since we recommend and take a lean approach to project management and training, the training team may create an ADDIE Design document template to help the design team get a quick start. Recall that templates can improve quality and reduce risk.

Design and development might not be completed until after testing is completed to ensure that training content and evaluation reflect the approved functionality and workflows (Figure II.3). Sometimes, the approved workflows change, especially in the testing phase if the workflow does not work as designed and the workflow changes. Therefore, instructional designers pay close attention to changes to approved workflows so that the content in training is aligned with workflows that have user acceptance testing approval (more about UAT later).

Training Goals and Objectives and Learning Outcomes

The instructional designer begins their ADDIE Design activities by reviewing the competency gaps, training goals and objectives, and learning outcomes identified and approved during the planning phase. One might consider the "target" training goals, objectives, and learning outcomes identified in the analysis phase as the performance gap and the solution outlined in the ADDIE Design process (Figure II.12).

While the training goals and objectives, and learning outcomes are identified during the planning phase, they are elaborated during the design phase. Instructional designers develop assessment activities to demonstrate competencies aligned with measurable learning outcomes.

Training goals: are broad and general statements about what the training program wishes to accomplish. Training goals are not easily measurable.

- Training goal example: understand how phishing works.

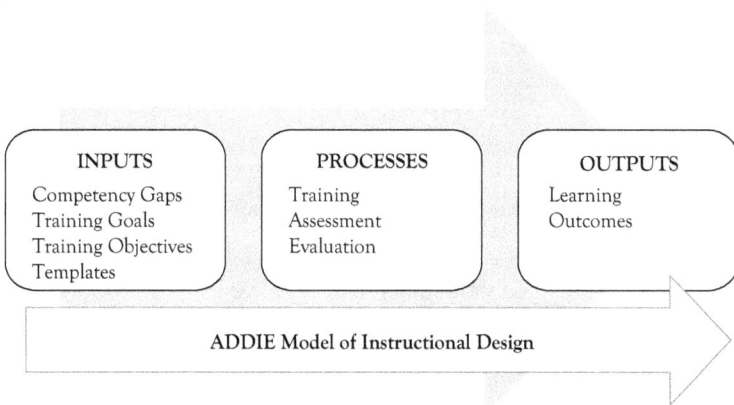

Figure II.12 Training and learning inputs, processes, and outputs

Training objectives: are derived from the training goals and are specific statements about what the instructor intends the learner can do because of the training.

- Training objective example: students will understand spear phishing, whaling, vishing, and e-mail phishing.

Learning outcomes: describe learning (the result, an output) due to training that can be demonstrated. Learning outcomes are measurable, and evidence learning has occurred. Learning outcomes differ from training objectives because they represent what was achieved by the learner rather than what was intended by the instructor (training objectives).

- Learning outcome example: The learner can explain the difference between spear phishing, whaling, vishing, and e-mail phishing ("explain" is mapped to Bloom's Taxonomy "Understand" level 2).

The instructional designer expands the learning outcomes to describe: (1) the new behavior after training, (2) the level of performance to be obtained after training, and (3) the environment in which the new competence will be used.

Thus, the instructional designer begins ADDIE Design activities by understanding competency gaps. They document training goals and objectives representing the intent of training while learning outcomes are focused on the training result. The instructional designer benefits from the clarity of documenting the training goals and objectives, and learning outcomes. Such documentation begins in the planning phase and is elaborated in the design phase with the project sponsor. While we illustrate the development flow as linear, it is our experience that developing training goals and objectives, and learning outcomes is a bit messy. However, collaborative iterations help to develop and elaborate coherent training goals and objectives and learning outcomes.

Learning Outcomes Alignment

Learning outcomes are what the learner can do because of training. Learning outcomes are like project deliverables (outputs); instructional designers make them measurable, objective, and achievable. We consider Bloom's Taxonomy when we develop learning outcomes (Table II.3) to improve quality. In *Cybersecurity Training*, we focus primarily on knowledge, comprehension, and application in cybersecurity general awareness and specialized training and less on higher-order cognitive thinking like synthesis and evaluation.

Training is designed to close competency gaps, and the instructional design process begins with identifying and aligning training goals, objectives, and learning outcomes. Before we move to training design, we pause and briefly examine how adults learn.

Microlearning

Since training goals and objectives, and learning outcomes form the foundation of any training program, there is considerable information and examples online to continue your learning:

- Aligning training goals and objectives and learning outcomes.
- Cybersecurity training goals and objectives and learning outcomes examples (refine your search by NIST and/or ISO examples).
- Training goals and objectives and learning outcomes templates.

Table II.3 Learning outcomes aligned with Bloom's Taxonomy

Bloom's Taxonomy	Learning outcome
Knowledge	List common cyber threats within the health care environment
Comprehension	Explain why the health care environment is a cybersecurity target
Application	Configure cybersecurity threat detection software
Analysis	Investigate the cybersecurity alerts report
Synthesis	Design a new cybersecurity threat architecture
Evaluation	Complete an evaluation of the five threat detection vendor bids

Andragogy: Study of Adult Learning

A critical success factor for well-designed cybersecurity training courses is to design instruction for the intended audience; our focus is on adults rather than children in *Cybersecurity Training*. Adults (andragogy) learn differently from children (pedagogy); teaching cybersecurity or technology-related skills to adults should also differ from teaching children.

Andra = Adult

Peda = Child

Adults are more successful at independent learning than children, who require more direction in the learning process. Adults acquire and learn from experience, while children have limited experiences and rely upon others to help them learn. Therefore, many cybersecurity training initiatives can benefit from a self-directed learning approach where learners can draw upon previous experience to learn new concepts. Learning is even more likely when the adult learner is ready to learn (e.g., just-in-time learning popularized in the 1990s) and ready to apply new skills and knowledge. Finally, adult learners are internally motivated to learn. Applying the principles of adult learning—andragogy—to any digital training program, including cybersecurity, can improve adult engagement and learning.

Learner Analysis

One of the early ADDIE Design activities the instructional designer completes is analyzing learners to understand the stakeholders and what they value regarding learning and training. Analyzing learners is a complex undertaking with multiple approaches and frameworks available. For example, Maslow's Hierarchy of Needs guides the instructional designer to address physical needs (e.g., a comfortable learning space) before higher-order needs can be met (e.g., learning new content). You may have seen in training that different pupils learn differently. Some people learn more effectively with graphs, pictures, and symbols (visual learners) or through listening (auditory learners). Others learn best through text-heavy content (reading learner) or a hands-on approach (kinesthetic learner). Sometimes, combining approaches can meet multiple learning styles and reinforce learning.

Analyzing learner needs within the NIST Cybersecurity Framework leads the instructional designer to analyze general awareness and specialized training. For these groups of learners, they may assess:

- *General characteristics*: examine the learner's age, culture, and cybersecurity experience.
- *Threshold competencies*: identify competencies required for learners to succeed in the proposed subject. Sometimes, prerequisite courses are required (e.g., general awareness training before specialized training).
- *Learning styles*: consider the learning styles (visual, auditory, reading, and kinesthetic) best suited for the instruction. For example, learning to secure hardware devices will be more successful if the theory is supplemented with hands-on exercises to secure hardware devices (e.g., one is unlikely to safely ride a motorcycle by only reading the owner's manual).
- *Learning obstacles:* examine any obstacles to learning like lack of commitment, lack of self-efficacy (belief in their ability), anxiety, distractions from business as usual, or restricted access to training. The project sponsor or line manager can help prevent or mitigate these risks.
- *Learner expectations:* determine what learners expect from the training. One way to gauge this effectively is to refer to the evaluations from prior organizational training data or lessons learned reports.
- *Self-assessment*: some types of learning benefit from a pretraining self-assessment and evaluation to better understand the current state and future competence. While there are pros (expedient) and cons (less likely to be honest and accurate) to self-assessments, NIST general awareness and specialized cybersecurity training generally do not require self-assessments.

Learner analysis, even when diligently following analytical procedures, is a best-guess exercise. Indeed, a generally accepted "best approach" to learner analysis does not exist. However, the NIST roles (e.g., privileged users, senior executives, etc.) offer discrete categories of learners that facilitate learner analysis.

Human-Centered Design

Have you ever used a product or followed a process that did not work well? Sometimes, products, services, and processes are efficient and effective but lack the human element to make them successful. The human-centered design movement is a design technique that places people at the center of the design process. Successful instructional designers involve the end users (learners and instructors) in an iterative design process that includes prototyping, feedback, refinement, and then release, followed by further improvements in the optimization phase. The human-centered design process (Figure II.13A) mirrors other iterative development processes, like the ADDIE Model of Instructional Design (Figure II.13B) and the scrum delivery process (Figure II.13C). The design team goes through familiar phases of discovering the challenges and defining the problem, followed by developing and delivering the solution.

Since these models begin with a demand for something and the process delivers a tangible product or service valued by the users, these iterative approaches benefit from project management tools (e.g., risk register and traceability matrix) and processes (e.g., risk, quality, and change management). Thus, the end users are engaged in the design workshops, prototyping, and testing. In the main project and the training subproject, instructional designers tailor, combine, and apply the project delivery and ADDIE approaches (Figure II.3).

Job Requirements Analysis

Some instructional designers may conduct a job requirements analysis on key cybersecurity jobs to understand role-based training requirements. Job analysis is a traditional activity in human resources management, and an HR specialist can help complete job analyses. To develop

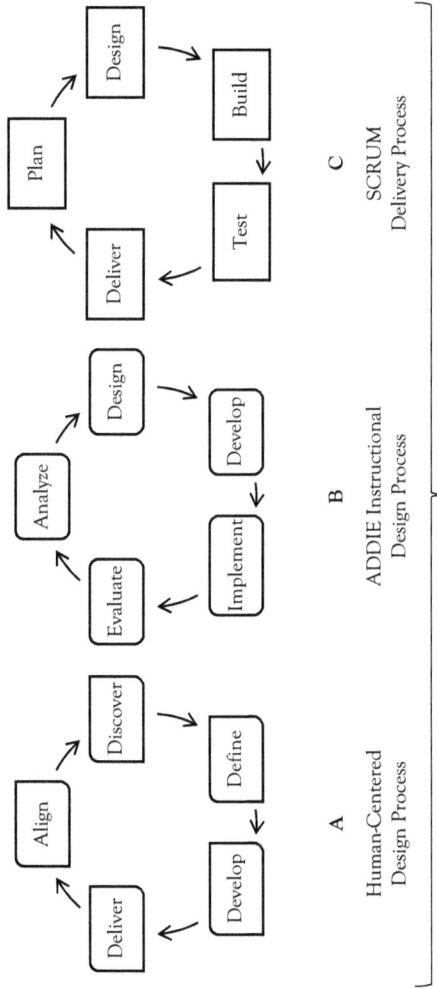

Iterative improvement is a natural way to progress and improve

A
Human-Centered
Design Process

B
ADDIE Instructional
Design Process

C
SCRUM
Delivery Process

Figure II.13 Iterative improvement processes

training requirements, the instructional designer analyzes jobs and tasks under operational conditions and performance standards. They leverage the NIST role-based training guides when analyzing jobs. Instructional designers work with the sponsor to prioritize job and task analysis according to learning criticality. They may use an agile technique to maintain a backlog of prioritized training requirements (Figure I.16). It is worth repeating that the training team collaborates with the training project sponsor to guide prioritization to deliver the proper cybersecurity awareness and specialized training.

However, we understand the challenges of conducting a job analysis, and the reader may not need this level of precision. Again, the instructional designer tailors, combines, and may use the structured job analysis method only for the most critical jobs.

Microlearning

There is a rich tradition of analyzing job requirements and ample resources online to support further study:

- What job analysis content is on the Society for Human Resource Management site?
- What is human-centered design?
- How can we use Robert Mager's criterion-referenced instruction framework?

Instructor Analysis

There will be some instances where instructor analysis can aid content development. For example, will the training be facilitated by an instructor? Will the training be face-to-face or online? Will the training be synchronous (teaching and learning occur simultaneously)? Or will teaching be asynchronous (teaching and learning do *not* occur simultaneously)? The training could be a self-directed subject where the learner watches an online lecture, with additional learning activities to reinforce learning. The instructional designer considers whether instructor training is required if the subject includes new technology (e.g., cybersecurity simulations).

Ideally, instructors can be invited to provide feedback throughout the ADDIE Model of Instructional Design process.

Plan the Instructional Methods

Some training projects can purchase training services like content, simulations, assessments, and outsourced instructors. Often, training materials are developed "in-house" by the organization and perhaps external partners/vendors. Learners become more engaged when multiple teaching approaches are used (e.g., lectures, simulations, and learning games). Engaged learners learn more. Therefore, we invite you to review instructional methods online to find additional techniques for your training. However, there are three common types of training methods to consider when planning training:

1. *Passive training:* Cybersecurity infographics on public monitor screens in organization passageways are increasingly used to deliver small bits of content. Cybersecurity tips for phishing prevention can be displayed on the employee's log-in screen. Optional pop-up quizzes can also be used to deliver content with the potential for small rewards. There are many ways to deliver successful passive training, especially with gamification techniques.

2. *Self-directed training:* The learner follows a guided learning path (e.g., completes a workbook or online training module). Often, there is an assessment (e.g., answer 10 multiple-choice questions using the LMS). Self-directed training through an LMS is appropriate for most cybersecurity awareness and specialized training. Specialized training may include online and face-to-face learning experiences for more advanced or impactful topics. Simulations or table-top execution cybersecurity "plays" (e.g., eradication and recovery) from your organization's cybersecurity incident and vulnerability response playbook are an effective way to learn, maintain competence, and achieve cybersecurity readiness, especially if lunch is provided!

3. *Face-to-face training:* The traditional approach to training is to have the instructor in the room with the student. Today, face-to-face training can be in-person or provided digitally. We and those

thought leaders we follow (see the *Testimonials* section in the front matter of this book) anticipate significant advancements in training with mature learning metaverse technologies. We introduce techniques later (ADDIE Develop section), like the flipped classroom that goes beyond traditional lecturing in a face-to-face setting. In a flipped classroom, students complete assigned readings and other learning activities before the training. The instructor briefly reviews the preparatory content and then guides the learners to apply the new learning to an authentic task. The advantage is that the trainer supports the learner, improving learning.

We invite you to develop a training implementation plan using project management tools and processes. We expand on the training implementation plan later in the Project Transition to Production (T2P) section.

Design Training

One of the early design decisions will be about the training modality; that is, what type of training is appropriate to address capacity gaps? Instructional designers begin early design discussions with the project sponsor; for example, they may discuss using the Box Car training approach (Figure II.11). While there are many ways to train, cybersecurity awareness and role-based training lend themselves to many standard training methods:

- *Instructor-led training*: Instructor-led training is the traditional approach that includes in-person training, online training, and blended learning. We describe blended learning as a combination of online and face-to-face learning interactions (and recognize that a "hard" or generally accepted definition of blended learning is elusive). A common approach is training occurs in the classroom with one instructor to many learners. Instructor-led training can also occur online, where the learners are distributed geographically, and a learning management system is used to support training. Blended learning brings together in-person learning with online elements. For example, the student may review online resources and complete an assignment before attending in-person learning with an instructor. The flipped classroom approach has the benefit that the learner prepares before the class, and when in the class, the instructor facilitates learning by having the students apply what they have learned to a problem presented in class. The learning management system (LMS) is used to distribute learning resources, record the in-class session for review, distribute and score the assessment, and record learner progress.

- *Self-directed learning*: Learners follow a lesson plan or curriculum to learn independently from an instructor. Microcredentials are a growing trend in higher education where courses are chunked into smaller, discrete subjects that a learner can complete quickly (e.g., 10 hours). The LMS may be used to distribute and score assessments and provide a place for learning resources. While this form of training is cost-effective, the main drawback is an instructor is not readily available. However, look for technology-driven support from bots and AI resources. The subject content may vary from a comprehensive course with multimedia learning resources and an assessment to a simple infographic to increase cybersecurity awareness. Self-directed learning is enhanced with digital badges that certify competency or accomplishment. Digital badges remain popular and are part of the emerging metaverse.

- *Train-the-trainer training*: The train-the-trainer approach is where someone from the learner's business unit provides training. Subject matter experts are taught how to train, assess, and evaluate. When new hires join their business unit, subject matter experts provide training in the new hire's specific role. The human resource-based trainer is unlikely to have such subject matter expertise. Therefore, the train-the-trainer method is a popular method of specialized training, beginning with general orientation, followed by role-based training. Some cybersecurity specialized training uses the train-the-trainer method.

- *Passive training*: One can passively provide cybersecurity learning opportunities with leaflets, e-mail games, computer wallpaper, and so on. For example, when employees receive a corporate e-mail about organizational news or a directive, the e-mail can end with questions about cybersecurity, innovation, customer service, or another component of culture targeted for strengthening. Points for correct answers are awarded and tracked on a leaderboard. E-mails can be gamified that help build and maintain organizational culture.

Part of the ADDIE Analysis phase is to analyze existing training materials for suitability or as a basis for modification. The sponsor can assist with evaluating existing materials to determine suitability or identify required revisions (e.g., the lean concept of reuse).

Instructional designers use chunking and scaffolding where appropriate to develop training materials. Chunking breaks up units into smaller pieces (chunking down), like in a work breakdown structure. Instructional designers consolidate fragments into a coherent, holistic construct (chunking up). Chunking is especially useful when we chunk content to help students progress through Bloom's Taxonomy levels. Indeed, one can design training activities where students draw from multiple levels of Bloom's Taxonomy.

Instructional designers understand that multiple methods of instruction and active learner engagement provide better learning retention than simple lectures (Figure II.14). The original research into learning retention rates (e.g., students retain 30 percent of what they learn when instruction is audiovisual-based) was appealing but controversial (Stice 2009).

The main criticism of the Learning Pyramid is the researchers proposed precise and even measurement of retention rates (e.g., 10 percent with reading, 20 percent with audiovisual, etc.) that other researchers could not replicate. While we may agree with the critics, the Learning Pyramid guides trainers to go beyond lectures and include more engaging teaching techniques like demonstrations, discussions, and simulations of the new task. For example, instructors might spend only a tiny amount of time lecturing and spend more time on highly engaging activities reflected

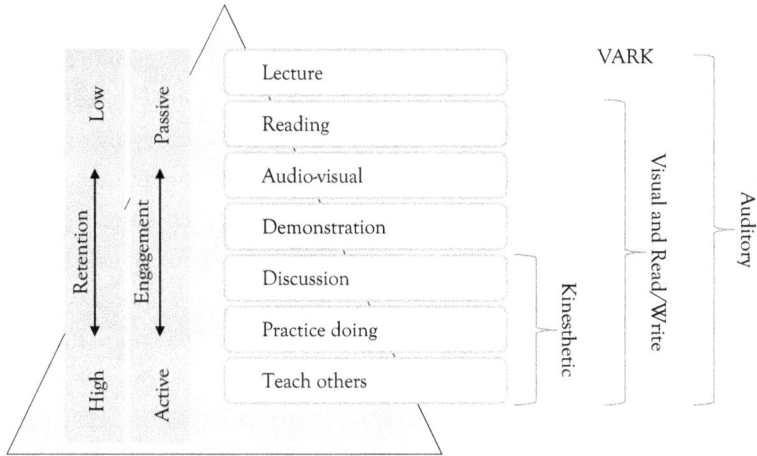

Figure II.14 Modified Learning Pyramid

in the larger area at the bottom of the triangle. In *Cybersecurity Training*, we ignore the retention debate and provide engaging learning experiences with simulations and gamification techniques. Increased engagement leads to increased learning.

The Learning Pyramid aligns with the VARK learning styles (e.g., kinesthetic) and how people learn best. While the VARK model of learning styles is not without criticism,[21] it reminds us to use multiple teaching techniques to increase learner engagement and learning outcome achievement. In our experience, bored students face learning barriers, while engaged students are more likely to learn. Therefore, we combine generally accepted models and best instructional design practices and tailor them to our purposes. For example, we use simulations and game-based learning in our instruction since these kinesthetic learning activities increase engagement and learning retention (Tews et al. 2020; Lester et al. 2023).

Instructional designers may develop two types of training materials: (1) learner-oriented (content, supplemental resources, exercises, and

---

[21] All models, frameworks, and theories have critics! Academics identify theoretical weaknesses (e.g., annotated literature reviews) and try to optimize. However, we can use theoretically sound elements of models, frameworks, and theories to improve practice.

evaluation instruments) and (2) the facilitator guide. Our attention thus far has been on the learner side of ADDIE; however, some training experiences can benefit from developing a facilitator guide to guide instruction. As the complexity of training and the impact of not learning increase, so do the formality and comprehensiveness of the facilitator guide.

The facilitator guide includes the training goals and objectives and learning outcomes as the bare minimum content. Instructional designers develop lesson plans that provide details about the lesson: classroom setup, content delivery instructions, in-class exercises, facilitation instructions or prompts (e.g., Socratic method of instruction), formative assessment details, activity time, resource list, preparation requirements, and so on. Often, facilitator guides have checklists to assure training quality: pretraining, training, and post-training. Some instructor checklists and guides include e-mail and other communication templates to improve communications. Facilitator guides are usually the last major training asset to be completed before delivering training. The facilitator guide should be included in the scope of pilot testing and assessed by an instructor likely to deliver the training (rather than by an instructional design guru on the project!).

Microlearning

Digital transformation is changing teaching and learning; emerging innovations can be found online and by signing up for the futurist's alerts:

- What are the emerging training technologies?
- Will robots replace teachers?
- How do flipped classrooms work?
- What are blended learning best practices?
- Are microcredentials worth it?
- What are the contents of a facilitator guide?

Training Templates

Recall that templates are tools to improve quality assurance and guide the user to complete a task. They reduce the time to complete the work

and simplify training document creation. They might also include branding and professional design elements or uniform contact information
(e.g., name, location, and contact details for the training team). You can
find templates online with instructions and examples. The instructions
and examples are deleted as the template is populated with the training project details. The organization may already have templates with
branding, or you may develop templates (hint: search online for freely
available training and project management templates for tailoring)
that align with our project-oriented approach to the ADDIE Model of
Instructional Design (Figure II.3), including:

- *Training plan template*: The training plan may include
  strategic and tactical elements. The training plan template
  allows space for training goals and objectives, the rationale
  for the training, the training project schedule with critical
  milestones (not the curriculum schedule for training), the
  training budget, resource plan, risk management plan,
  procurement plan, and so on. Some training projects will
  require a fully populated template, while others might leave
  some template sections blank (e.g., "Procurement: Not
  applicable as only internal resources are used." It is good
  practice to explain why the section of the template is "not
  applicable."). Instructional designers tailor the template to
  achieve a lean training plan with sufficient quality and risk
  management.
- *Learning needs assessment template*: Templates can guide the
  learning needs analysis process and might be included in the
  training plan.
- *Training goals, objectives, and outcomes template*: Instructional
  designers include a definition of training goals, objectives, and
  learning outcomes in the template instructions with examples
  to guide the template user. A content developer can follow a
  template to develop training goals, objectives, and learning
  outcomes into their training products and services.
- *Subject outline*: The subject outline template is like a contract
  between the learner and the training organization. A subject

is one unit of instruction (e.g., Advanced Risk Management), and a course is a program of subjects (e.g., a four-part module for a cybersecurity technical role). Some organizations provide detailed descriptions of their subjects and include the following:

o Subject name;
o Subject identification information (e.g., subject code, category, level, etc.);
o Prerequisites;
o Delivery mode (online, face-to-face, independent learning, etc.);
o Subject developer's name and contact information;
o Subject sponsor and business unit;
o Cost center;
o Academic integrity statement;
o Subject description;
o Subject and program learning outcomes;
o Subject content overview;
o Learning is assessed: yes/no;
o Assessment and evaluation overview (e.g., a final multiple-choice exam);
o Assignment description, individual or group work, and timing;
o Subject delivery information (frequency, class length, personal study hours, etc.);
o Resource list (e.g., *Quantum Cybersecurity: A Transition Plan* book);
o Document version control details;
o And so on.

Subject (and course) outlines improve service delivery for busy training departments. Developing and managing the subject outline catalog aligns with ITIL service catalog management. You can enhance your subject catalog with training templates to assure quality and reduce risks:

- *Lesson plan template*: The lesson plan template provides a quick start to planning each day or shorter training sessions. Some lesson plans can include multiple days of training. Lesson plans are like a roadmap detailing what will be done and how it will be done during the learning experience, such as listing training goals and objectives and learning outcomes, main content, key resources, and so on.

- *Pilot test template*: The main steps in pilot testing include planning the pilot test, preparing the environment, conducting the pilot test, evaluating, revising, and scaling up for delivery.

- *Training communications template*: The training team uses templates to inform end users of upcoming training. A standard error in corporate communications is to omit essential information such as the date, time, or location, and templates help achieve completeness. The training team may also develop communication templates to inform end users how to access additional support during the go-live period.

- *Trainer onboarding template*: Onboarding guidelines quickly integrate new team members onto their projects. We recommend and include the project charter from the main project and other information typical to onboarding, such as expectations, training culture and philosophy, values and principles, contact information, and so on, when we bring new team members onto our projects. Recall templates improve quality.

- *Pretraining checklist template*: The checklist may include confirmation activities (e.g., confirm the location, date, time, etc.), classroom setup on the day of training activities, technology setup activities (e.g., passwords, training environment, etc.), and other checklist items like catering.

- *Reaction template*: The reaction template is another commonly used training template that can be tailored depending on the type of training. The reaction template will include questions to collect data about whether learners liked the class, whether it was a good use of time and met their training needs, and so on. Reaction templates are often included in an LMS subject and may be disabled if not required. Reaction data can be a lessons learned input.

- *Rubric template*: Rubrics are a tool used to evaluate and score the students' work against criteria (e.g., the learner can describe the common "respond" steps for a cybersecurity incident). Rubrics are usually built into learning management systems as core functionality. However, rubric templates are helpful in the design phase and can include examples to help the instructional designer get a quick start. We more fully address rubrics in our evaluation section.

Training templates are quality assurance tools that can improve quality and reduce risks while allowing a quick project start. We love templates, and there seem to be valuable templates online for almost everything!

Design Evaluation Program

In *Cybersecurity Training*, we apply the concept of the *chain of impact* where training is process-based, beginning with the demand for training, training development, training delivery (Figure II.3), and the transfer of learning to the job to benefit the organization (Figure I.4). We embed a project-oriented approach with the ADDIE Model of Instructional Design. We use the Kirkpatrick Model of Evaluation for its rigor, adaptability, and other benefits like helping to delineate in scope and out of scope evaluations.

Evaluation is a process, and processes can be improved. Therefore, the instructional design team may start the evaluation design with a quick lessons learned discussion to optimize the current project:

- What worked well in previous evaluations?
- What can be improved in the evaluation process and with artifacts and templates?

Too often, lessons learned are conducted at the end of the project when it is too late to apply them to the current project. Therefore, we recommend and conduct brief and informal lessons learned discussions at the *beginning* of each project phase to improve our practice in the current project.

Learning evaluation design begins after a review of training goals and objectives and learning outcomes to assure evaluation alignment (hint: develop a one-page document that lists training goals and objectives, and learning outcomes to keep the instructional design team and sponsor focused and aligned).

Guided by lean thinking, instructional designers develop a bare minimum learning evaluation. Additional *Fact Sheets* or *bots* can be developed later to support less-used system functionality. Much of the NIST cybersecurity awareness and training content usually aligns with the lower levels of Bloom's Taxonomy (e.g., knowledge, comprehension, and application). The higher levels of Bloom's Taxonomy (e.g., analysis, synthesis, and evaluation) can be addressed in professional development and cybersecurity education per the NIST Cybersecurity Learning Continuum (Figure I.12). The instructional design team will develop assessments appropriate for the type of NIST training required when considering Bloom's Taxonomy.

Evaluation is related to quality control: "find and fix defects." The purpose of evaluation in the ADDIE Model of Instructional Design is to determine the level or degree of training success. Test items are written to measure learner performance for each learning outcome. The instructional designer and instructor evaluate whether the learner has learned and how training can be improved. If training is unsuccessful, changes like remediation (re-training to develop the desired competencies) or making changes to the instructional materials may be implemented.

Recall that continual improvement, including evaluation, is central to *Cybersecurity Training*; instructional designers continually evaluate learning and training activities along the project management and ADDIE processes (Figure II.3). Therefore, instructional designers think and apply continual improvement to cybersecurity training activities.

Notice that evaluation and assessment have similar meanings. In *Cybersecurity Training*, we use "assessment" when the focus is on collecting data for evaluation purposes. We use "evaluation" to measure student performance using assessment data. While assessment and evaluation are companion activities, a researcher may consider assessment as data collection and evaluation as data analysis.

Assessment = Data Collection
Evaluation = Data Analysis

Microlearning

Assessing and evaluating learning are rooted in quality management theory and practice and are detailed in ISO standards:

- Search online for an overview of the ISO 9001 Quality Management Systems standard.
- How is the ISO 19001 Auditing Management Systems standard organized? The ISO Auditing Management standard outlines generally accepted auditing processes, practices, and principles that can be tailored to learning assessment and evaluation.

Kirkpatrick Model of Evaluation

A companion process to teaching is learning evaluation. While there are other models of evaluation, the Kirkpatrick Model of Evaluation (Figure II.15) is the most popular: "One of the most cited approaches to summative evaluation in [instructional design] is Kirkpatrick's Four Levels of Evaluation. Kirkpatrick developed this model to evaluate the effectiveness of training programs—specifically, training programs in industry" (Brown and Green 2016, 172). We use and recommend the Kirkpatrick Model of Evaluation to determine the success of general awareness and specialized training as outlined in *Cybersecurity Training*.

Evaluation specialists may evaluate skills, knowledge, and attitudes, usually after the training intervention, to determine if the desired changes have occurred (e.g., to identify a deep fake message from your manager) as part of a cybersecurity general awareness training capability. Evaluation determines the degree to which learning outcomes have been achieved due to the learning experience.

Kirkpatrick Evaluation			
1 Reaction	**2** Learning	**3** Behavior	**4** Results
Did you enjoy the training? Was the training practical? Was it a good use of your time? What did you think of the training facility? Did the technology help or hinder learning? Was the training easy? Were you comfortable? Do you have any recommendations?	Did the participants learn what was intended according to the learning outcomes? Did the learner have the desired learning experience? To what degree did the learner develop new competencies?	Did the learners apply what they learned to their work? What competencies were used? Was the learning and change in behavior sustained? Did the learner transfer the new competency to another setting?	How will the benefits be measured? (For example, relate training impact to cybersecurity KPIs like Mean Time To Detect and Mean Time To Resolve. Compare pre- and post-training KPIs.)
Project Scope		Business Scope	

LOW ⟶ Evaluation Difficulty Increases ⟶ HIGH

Figure II.15 Kirkpatrick Model of Evaluation

Most NIST-aligned evaluations will be criterion-referenced rather than norm-referenced. Evaluations that determine levels of competence against specific criteria are criterion-referenced; learning gaps can then be identified and remediated. Comparing learners to other learners is a norm-referenced evaluation and not typically part of a NIST training evaluation.

Learning Evaluation Scope

Our evaluation model in *Cybersecurity Training* aligns with the Kirkpatrick Model, ADDIE Model of Instructional Design, and the hybrid project delivery approach: instructional designers identify the in scope and out of scope evaluation activities, develop a schedule, use the change

In Scope   Out-of-Scope
Project Responsibility   Business Responsibility

Training Need	Reaction	Learning	Application	Organizational Impact

Business Strategy	Evaluation Instrument:	Evaluation Instrument:	Self-Report	Attitudinal Survey
Audit Finding	Multiple-Choice	Multiple-Choice	Manager Report	Net Promoter Score
Severe Incident	Likert Scale	Likert Scale	Observation	
	Automated Scoring	Automated Scoring	360° Feedback	

Kirkpatrick Evaluation

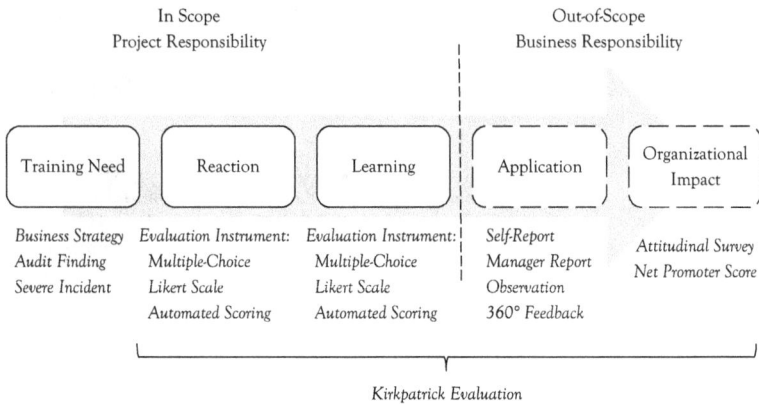

Figure II.16 Project-oriented model of evaluation

control and risk management processes, and so on (Figure II.16). The
training project manager elaborates the training need with the project
sponsor (e.g., an audit identified competency gaps). The instructional
design team may evaluate the learners' reactions to the training and what
they learned. After the student leaves the learning experience, learning
may be evaluated by the learner's supervisor (e.g., through direct obser-
vation). Measuring the impact of training on the organization is desirable but usually out of scope for the training team. The project-oriented
model of evaluation also illustrates elements of the learning chain of
impact, beginning with a training need, the learning experience with the
transfer of learning, and impact measurement to the organization.

One analyzes the training objectives against Bloom's Taxonomy to
develop appropriate learning evaluations (Figure II.17). Recall that training objectives are what your organization intends to do, and learning outcomes are the new learning due to the learning experience. The instructional
designer matches the cognitive level of complexity (Bloom's Taxonomy)
with the evaluation technique (e.g., multiple choice, short answer, test plan

Training Objectives	Bloom's Taxonomy	Evaluation

Figure II.17 Evaluation alignment

development). Therefore, the instructional designers seek training objectives alignment with an evaluation, which is helped by using Bloom's Taxonomy.

Bloom's Taxonomy guides the appropriate types of evaluation for each hierarchical level of learning (Table II.4). For example, some specialized training (Security Architect) requires knowledge of cybersecurity-related regulations related to their industry (e.g., HIPAA for health care or the CPS 234 Information Security Prudential Standard for Australian deposit-taking institutions like banks and general insurers). The instructional designer writes multiple-choice questions to evaluate knowledge of regulations. Higher-order learning is applying knowledge successfully, like constructing and configuring technical devices aligned with cybersecurity standards or frameworks. In this case, multiple-choice questions would not be the best evaluation instrument; instead, the instructor may ask the learner to demonstrate smart IoT device configuration according to NIST IoT guidelines and use a checklist to assess and evaluate the learner's competence.

Finally, one moves up Bloom's Taxonomy when the learner is required to demonstrate evaluation capabilities; for example, IT security SMEs (NIST specialized training) may be required to evaluate cybersecurity governance with a one-page written answer that would be evaluated by the instructor using a rubric.

Rubrics are evaluation instruments with specific criteria to determine the learner's performance. The instructor tallies the individual criterion scores using the LMS rubric to arrive at an overall score representing the degree of competence. The rubric includes performance descriptors for

Table II.4 Evaluation analysis

Instructional objectives	Bloom's Taxonomy level	Evaluation examples
Identify legal aspects related to patient data	Knowledge	Multiple-choice questions about HIPAA privacy and security legislation
Construct and configure an IoT device compliant with current cybersecurity guidelines	Application	Use a checklist to evaluate the configuration against the NIST IoT guidelines
Evaluate governance procedures for protecting systems from ransomware attacks	Evaluation	Use a rubric to evaluate the learner's choice of ransomware procedures against NIST Cybersecurity Framework best practices

Table II.5 Rubric example with Bloom's Taxonomy levels

Instructional objective	Role	Emerging	Competent	Expert
Examine the waterfall and agile delivery approaches as they relate to software security	Software Developer	COMPREHENSION: explain the waterfall, agile, and DevSecOps delivery approaches relationship to software security	ANALYZE: examine the waterfall, agile, and DevSecOps delivery approaches to software security	CREATE: design secure software with the DevSecOps delivery approaches
Execute security testing scripts for IoT software	Testing and Evaluation Specialist	COMPREHENSION: explain generic IoT testing procedures	APPLY: execute security testing scripts for IoT software	EVALUATE: appraise your IoT security testing process
Describe the elements that impact an organization's cybersecurity	Authorizing Official or Designating Representative	COMPREHENSION: identify elements that impact an organization's cybersecurity	UNDERSTAND: explain the elements that impact an organization's cybersecurity	APPLY: illustrate the elements that impact an organization's cybersecurity

each level of competence. While a rubric is like a rating scale, the rubric has more descriptive language (Table II.5). Rubrics are as varied as evaluations; they often include proficiency levels (e.g., emerging, competent, and expert) for the criterion under review (e.g., instructional objective). For illustrative purposes, our rubric includes various cybersecurity roles for evaluating the instructional objective. However, each role should have its unique set of rubrics to evaluate competence. Each major assessment item (e.g., creating a design or a policy) will have a rubric to assess learning outcomes. Instructional designers may tailor rubrics by adding more detail for critical competencies and less for less impactful learning. Well-designed rubrics contribute to valid and reliable evaluations.

After the rubric is developed, its alignment with the learning outcomes is verified. During the pilot study, the instructional designer evaluates whether the rubric is "fit for purpose" with other training assets to find and fix defects and get sponsor approval.

Developing valid and reliable evaluation instruments requires specialized knowledge and can be improved through practice. Multiple-choice questions are suitable for assessing learning outcomes for most cybersecurity awareness and specialized training. Many experts offer multiple-choice instrument development guidelines (Brown and Green 2016):

1. What is the purpose of the evaluation?
2. Who will be evaluated? (e.g., general awareness training for everyone or specialized training)
3. How long is the assessment?
4. What will the assessment cover?
5. What content will be used?
6. Will there be a test pool of assessment items? How many items are in the test pool (e.g., 36 multiple-choice questions)? How many items will be drawn from the test pool (e.g., 10 multiple-choice questions and answers, randomly chosen to reduce the probability of successful cheating)?
7. What is the appropriate degree of difficulty (e.g., Bloom's Taxonomy)?
8. How will the assessment items be sequenced (e.g., randomly, so my question 6 is your question 12)?
9. How will the items be scored?

10. How will the test be evaluated (e.g., manually or automatically by the learning management system)?
11. Will a postassessment analysis be conducted (e.g., item analysis or lessons learned)?

These considerations can be converted into an evaluation template to aid assessment and evaluation design.

Constructed response questions (also known as open-ended) are helpful when there is not necessarily one correct answer. These long-answer questions can be used in higher-order learning to assess the "evaluate" and "create" categories of Bloom's Taxonomy. Essay questions are the most common type of constructed response questions. One can supplement multiple-choice questions with constructed response questions for NIST specialized training assessments. However, evaluating constructed response questions takes longer and is not required for most cybersecurity awareness and specialized training.

One can also determine skill development through training and use evaluation techniques like direct testing, performance rating, observations, and portfolios to gauge whether the skill has been developed. Direct testing involves evaluating whether the learner can perform the skill (e.g., conduct system security testing on a mobile and IoT device). The evaluation may use qualitative performance ratings where the learner's performance ability is given a grade (e.g., Developing, Average, or Excellent). One can also use a checklist to determine whether individual skill components have been sufficiently developed. Performance rating assessment templates with instructions for use improve interrater reliability so that two evaluators will have the same performance rating. Finally, portfolios illustrate a learner's capabilities and are suitable for evaluating complex thinking (e.g., for specialist roles).

Microlearning

To determine whether learning occurred, the instructor assesses and evaluates; therefore, those involved with training are rewarded by deepening their knowledge and understanding of these foundational concepts. The reader can find more about adult learning assessment and evaluation online.

- How do rubrics work?
- What is the difference between criterion-referenced and normative assessments?
- What is the difference between validity and reliability?
- What is a constructed response question?
- How to improve interrater reliability?
- What new LMS assessment tools are emerging?

Formative Assessment

Formative assessment monitors student learning throughout training and before the final assessment (summative assessment); it is like regularly taking the pulse of learning during the learning experience. Assessment may also occur before training as a preinstruction (baseline) assessment. Baseline assessments are not generally required for general awareness and specialized cybersecurity training in the NIST Cybersecurity Framework. A preinstruction evaluation can be used as a baseline to determine the amount of learning due to the learning experience (e.g., evaluate a change in attitude toward cybersecurity). Instructors use formative assessments to determine whether the training is successful *during* the instruction or learning experience. One can take corrective actions during training if formative assessment indicates learning is off track.

Summative Assessment

Summative assessment occurs when the learning experience is *finished*, and the learner's achievement is assessed against learning outcomes (e.g., criterion-referenced assessment). As cybersecurity learning criticality increases, one is justified to adopt more rigorous and comprehensive assessments (both formative and summative).

Well-designed assessments can provide data that allow the trainer to evaluate the degree learning outcomes have been attained and what needs to be done if learning falls short.

While instructional designers apply formative and summative Kirkpatrick evaluations, they also pursue continual improvement opportunities within the ADDIE process. For example, instructional designers look to remove obsolete or irrelevant content due to changing roles and workflows.

Question Development

We recommend and use multiple-choice and Likert scale questions for most cybersecurity training rather than open-ended (constructed response) questions. Open-ended questions (e.g., explain the detection function's role in information privacy) can provide deep learning insights but require more effort to evaluate than multiple-choice and Likert scale questions. Multiple-choice questions are an effective evaluation instrument when correctly written (e.g., avoid trick and double-negative questions). Many multiple-choice question development resources online help instructional designers develop valid and reliable evaluations.

Likert scale questions offer a range of answers to a statement to record the learner's reaction to the frequency, quality, intensity, agreement, approval, awareness, importance, familiarity, satisfaction, and performance (Figure II.18, and later in Reaction Evaluation Design). Designing Likert questions can be challenging as the instructional designer has wide latitude. For example, will there be an even or odd number of choices? Odd number Likert choices allow the learner to select a middle ground where even-numbered Likert scales force the learner to choose a position (e.g., there is no "undecided" in a 4-point Likert scale). More choices (seven versus five) provide more accurate data but also come with the burden of additional analysis. Ultimately, providing fewer choices and keeping it simple produces compelling and easily managed evaluation datasets. Sometimes, emojis can improve understanding, resulting in fewer errors. However, assessing the range of agreement has limited use; for example, Likert scale questions are helpful for reaction types of questions and for assessing the lower levels of understanding according to Bloom's Taxonomy.

Open-ended questions (e.g., constructed response questions like "explain how you would design and secure virtual environments for

5 Point Likert Scale

Extremely Helpful	Very Helpful	Somewhat Helpful	Not So Helpful	Not At All Helpful

7 Point Likert Scale

Totally Hackable	Hackable	Slightly Hackable	Neutral	Slightly Protected	Protected	Perfectly Protected

4 Point Likert Scale

Strongly Disagree	Disagree	Agree	Strongly Agree

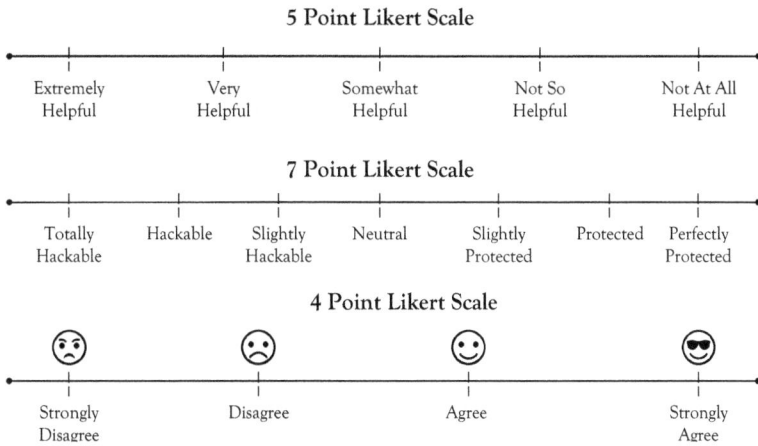

Figure II.18 Likert scale evaluation

testing?") assess higher levels of cognitive thought in Bloom's Taxonomy, like "analysis," but require considerably more effort to evaluate.

Most learning management systems have multiple-choice and Likert scale capabilities, automatic scoring, and training records management. The instructor does not have to manually score the evaluation and record the results in the learner's training file. Evaluating the transfer of learning and training impact on the organization is usually out of scope for the training project team. Transfer of learning and organizational impact is the responsibility of the training sponsor or someone like the learner's line manager.

Microlearning

The discipline of assessment and evaluation has a long tradition buoyed by rich research (qualitative, quantitative, and mixed methods) with practical examples online:

- What are the best practices for writing multiple-choice questions?
- What are the best practices for writing Likert scale questions?
- When should multiple-choice questions be avoided?
- How do students cheat with online exams?

Evaluation Baseline

Some training theorists recommend establishing a competency baseline before training to determine the degree of learning due to training (baseline evaluation—train—evaluate learning). However, the purpose of cybersecurity learning evaluation is not to demonstrate the degree of change but to determine whether the learner has acquired cybersecurity knowledge and skills. Therefore, instructional designers do not generally conduct baseline evaluations for NIST general awareness and role-based training. Instead of putting organizational effort into baseline competency evaluations, the organization may receive a potentially greater return on investments from practicing cybersecurity incident remediation actions as outlined in the organization's cybersecurity incident and vulnerability response playbooks.

Evaluation Timing

Instructional designers consider the timing of evaluation: "when should we assess?" In *Cybersecurity Training*, we recommend and evaluate project performance throughout the entire project (e.g., capture feedback and conduct lessons learned). We also evaluate learning throughout the learning chain of impact (Figure II.3). We evaluate training and learning (Kirkpatrick reaction and learning levels 1 and 2) as close to the training event as possible to increase evaluation validity. However, some newly learned skills might rarely be used and deteriorate over time (e.g., first aid and defibrillator skills for a cardiac arrest). While behavioral evaluation (e.g., the application of learning to one's job) is potentially the most valuable type of evaluation, the learner might not be required to apply the new competency for a significant period, making Kirkpatrick's higher levels of evaluation challenging.

Evaluator

Who should evaluate training and learning? Usually, the trainer evaluates learning (reaction, formative, and summative) as they are likely subject matter experts and can immediately address any learning gaps.

The instructional design team may use the learning management system to configure automatic scoring and records management for cybersecurity awareness and role-based evaluations. The instructional designers might include an LMS learner reaction questionnaire template automatically available within the LMS classroom. Instructors building LMS classrooms can use the template to capture learners' feedback about the training (e.g., the trainer does not have to create their reaction assessment themselves). Lessons learned about the training project can be led by the training lead or the project manager. The training sponsor or the line manager can evaluate the transfer of learning to the job.

The project stakeholders, including the training team collectively (Figures II.5 and II.6), determine project success; indeed, different stakeholders may have different perspectives (e.g., the training was successful, but the procurement process can be improved). The organizational impact from training is difficult to assess reliably and accurately; therefore, organizational impact assessments are left to others. However, the training team is interested in measuring the link between training and organizational performance as quantitative metrics can bolster the importance of training contribution (e.g., cybersecurity training return on investment—ROI) to organizational performance to justify their training budgets.

Reaction Evaluation Design

Evaluating at the reaction level serves the purpose of understanding what the learner thought and felt about the end-to-end training process, including the training intervention. "Reactionnaires" are often distributed as the final training activity to ensure a high response rate. We value and recommend reaction-level evaluations as they can serve a quality control purpose, for example, improving the training registration process. Training becomes leaner when defects or process "pain points" are removed or minimized. However, some researchers have criticized reaction-level evaluations as the relationship between reaction-level evaluations and transfer of learning was weak in some studies. Indeed, learners can confuse an excellent presentation delivered by a dynamic instructor with self-reported learning.

Kirkpatrick encourages instructional designers to conduct reaction-level evaluations because they want the learners to return (Kirkpatrick 1983). We also encourage and use reaction-based assessments in our practice as they are a form of lessons learned. We use a 4-point Likert questionnaire (Figure II.18) regarding four categories: (1) overall quality of the training, (2) quality of the instructor, (3) quality of the materials, and (4) quality of the learning environment. We pose questions for each of these four categories tailored to the specific learning experience: (1) "How could the training be improved?" (2) "How could the instructor improve their delivery?" (3) "How could the materials be made more useful?" and (4) "What changes could be made to the environment to make it more conducive to learning?" Learners use an LMS system to answer the four questions.

While reaction-level training often focuses on subject administration (e.g., was the registration process simple? etc.), there are opportunities to collect data to improve the learning experience:

- *Difficulty*: Some researchers have related learners' perceptions of subject difficulty with decreased learning. Therefore, the instructional designer needs to "scaffold" the lesson so that the learner succeeds with progressively more complex material at a comfortable pace. Early successes provide learner confidence, encourage engagement, and promote additional learning. If the learners find the training difficult, then there is a risk that less learning may occur. Scaffolding helps to improve the learner's self-efficacy (ability to learn and achieve their goals). One can add a 4-point Likert question: "The training was not overly difficult." The Likert feedback is returned to the instructional designer for optimization. For example, if 71 percent of the respondents either "agreed or strongly agreed" that the training was difficult, then the instructional designer would conclude the training might be too difficult for some and will further investigate. Reaction-level feedback can be used to improve training quality.
- *Sequencing*: Poor sequencing can negatively affect engagement and learning, like the inappropriate degree of content

difficulty. Therefore, we can write a Likert statement to determine if changes should be made to content sequencing in the training program to improve scaffolding: "The training was logical." If 88 percent of the respondents either "agreed or strongly agreed" that the training was logical, then the instructional designer would conclude the training sequence is suitable for most learners in that cohort and will not act.

- *Training aids*: Instructional designers seek learners' opinions about training aids (e.g., simulations, leaderboards, handouts, microlearning, etc.) because adults learn better when multiple teaching approaches are used (visual, auditory, reading, writing, and kinesthetic). Therefore, instructional designers may single out each learning aid and ask questions like: "Was the leaderboard engaging?" Again, using the 4-point Likert scale, the instructional designer might learn that 96 percent either "agreed or strongly agreed" that the leaderboard was engaging during the learning process. They conclude the learning probability was improved with engaged learners and may continue to use leaderboards and other gamification techniques in their practice.

Instructional designers are cautious not to include too many evaluation items: more evaluation items increase the amount of information we receive but also can discourage the learner from completing the assessment if there are "too many" evaluation items. Gamification techniques can increase assessment completion (e.g., add encouragement messages to the survey like "60% Survey Completion: Great Job! Or Keep Going! Only Three Questions Remain").

Learning Evaluation Design

Evaluating learning is a challenging endeavor with varied expert opinions. While we appreciate the intellectual rigor behind the art and science of evaluating learning, we favor a lean approach that can deliver quick results but perhaps with less precision appropriate for most NIST general awareness and specialized training. Most general awareness and specialized training align with the lower levels of Bloom's Taxonomy (Figure I.3) and, therefore, do not require advanced assessment techniques; more advanced cybersecurity topics (Figure I.12) can benefit from precise, comprehensive, and multifaceted assessments.

When instructional designers evaluate Kirkpatrick's "learning" level two (Figure II.15), they strive to measure the amount of competency attainment (e.g., skills, knowledge, attitude, etc.) due to training. They use learning management system assessment tools to write multiple-choice and Likert questions. An early consideration is the degree of assessment thoroughness: Is the assessment a simple, five-minute assessment, or is it much more comprehensive? Again, the impact of not learning informs instructional designers about the thoroughness of the assessment.

Instructional designers conduct a simple risk assessment to guide assessment design. For high-risk content (e.g., a high probability the learner will require the content, and if the content is not mastered, then the impact is high), the assessment is likely to be comprehensive (Figure II.19). Based on a risk assessment of the NIST training (e.g., awareness or specialized), the instructional designer and IT security can identify the impact on the organization if insufficient learning occurs and may recommend a more thorough evaluation. Each organization is different, and organizations change through time; therefore, there is no universally correct answer to "how thorough should NIST general awareness and specialized evaluations be?"

We take and generally recommend a lean approach and apply the minimum viable assessment (e.g., agile's minimum viable product) that is appropriate for the level of impact of not learning, expanding the assessment as appropriate.

Intuitively, the instructional designer knows a learner's performance during training may be an unreliable predictor of future performance.

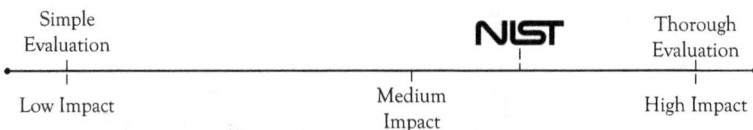

Figure II.19 Assessment coverage continuum

For example, the "out-of-air procedure" in scuba diving may work well in the training pool but might be poorly executed a year or two after the training in a real diving emergency at 28 meters in the Straits of Titan, Egypt. Therefore, instructional designers prudently and tactfully discuss this learning degradation risk with the sponsor to prevent (e.g., regular practice) and mitigate (coaching and/or remedial training) if necessary. Therefore, the Kirkpatrick Model goes beyond learning and includes behavior transfer to the job level (Figure II.15).

Microlearning

Evaluation is core to assessing learning, and you can learn more by searching online:

- What are key adult learning evaluation principles?
- What is high-impact learning?
- Should we stop assessing learning?

Design Constraints

The instructional designer is advised to consider design constraints (equipment, budget, schedule, technology, and human resources) and address them through the project risk and issue management process. Related to design constraints is team conflict; constraints often pressure teams, leading to conflict. Conflict avoidance can proactively be managed through team formation and conflict resolution strategies (e.g., project managers proactively try to avoid or minimize Tuckman's "storming" phase of team development).

Learning Management System Design

The learning management system (LMS) can be designed to support the training strategy, plan, and design. Learning prioritization (must have, should have, and would be nice categories) can guide the instructional design team so the most critical training needs are satisfied. Unmet training requests can be prioritized for a future date using the product backlog in continual improvement (Figure I.20). An instructional designer may create simple classrooms for others to use and modify with optional built-in functionality (e.g., reaction surveys). An instructor can use the built-in classroom (rather than starting from "scratch") and configure it to support their assigned subject. Like project management templates that allow a quick start, instructional designers develop ready-made LMS classrooms with optional LMS functionality that is useful to most instructors and learners. For example, instructors may use a leaderboard that comes with their classrooms; if the subject is long enough, they use this powerful gamification technique that increases learner engagement. Likewise, the instructor may turn off the optional leaderboard functionality for a short course. However, leaderboards can be used to track learning progress throughout the year with the successful completion of each subject or learning activity. Thus, instructional designers develop minimum viable classrooms with optional functionality for others to get a quick start on classroom building.

The instructional designer may discuss with the sponsor what learning materials are required and how to satisfy the demand for training. To support learning, the instructional designer may add resources (e.g., the NIST Cybersecurity Framework document) to their LMS classrooms.

Instructional designers set up and schedule assessments (formative and summative) in the LMS using multiple-choice and Likert questions with automatic scoring. When the learner has finished the assessment, the answers are automatically scored and posted to the student's learning record as completion evidence of general awareness, cybersecurity, and specialized training. The training manager can use the LMS to generate training and evaluation reports for compliance and human resource purposes.

Training Registration

The ADDIE Model training plan may include information about the enrollment process—a potentially challenging endeavor made easier with a learning management system. As the training project team progresses toward go-live, they increase the granularity of planning (also known as "rolling wave planning"). Often, high-level plans are agreed upon, but with subsequent planning, there may be challenges related to the process or technology requiring plan adjustments. Ideally, the pilot study will identify any registration challenges for the training team to remedy. Several pilot study considerations will require stakeholder discussion:

1. How will enrollment be managed? A customer relationship management system, a learning management system, or another method?
2. Who enrolls the learner? The training manager, the unit manager, the learner, or someone else?
3. Is the training mandatory or optional?
4. When does the training have to be completed? Is the training recurring where the learner must repeat the training annually (e.g., organizational health and safety training, code of ethics, general awareness and cybersecurity refresher, etc.)?
5. What happens if the learner does not attend or fails the evaluation? Who is responsible for enforcing this policy?
6. Is at-the-shoulder support required for the go-live period? Some technologies and new concepts are more successfully applied when supports are immediately available (a scaffolding principle) so that the learner has early success with the new technology or concepts. During the go-live stand-up meetings, at-the-shoulder support, learning adoption, and transfer can be agenda items. At-the-shoulder support combined with a central command center are strategies that ease new learning adoption and transfer. At-the-shoulder support is helpful for some role-based learning (e.g., configuring new detection software). Add this at-the-shoulder service to T2P communications where appropriate.

The training registration process can be time-consuming if it is manually managed. Therefore, try to automate the training registration process where possible.

Risk Management

Training projects, like other projects, face risks and issues. Therefore, in *Cybersecurity Training*, instructional designers use project risk management tools and processes to deliver exceptional learning experiences. They start with the ADDIE Model of Instructional Design and elaborate on the training goals and objectives, and learning outcomes. Professionals from all industries and disciplines reduce risk by aligning with standards and frameworks like the ADDIE Model of Instructional Design. Pilot testing before going live is another risk management technique and helps prevent flawed training.

We recommend and use project risk management practices and tools in all our projects, including training to improve the probability of success. In *Shields Up: Cybersecurity Project Management*, proven risk management techniques are detailed that improve the probability of project success, including training projects. Projects fail because risks become issues; therefore, risk management is the key to successful projects.

Design-Phase Outputs

The design phase concludes when "enough" of the design is complete. Project teams use the concept of "rolling wave design," where they try not to include all design details since they may change as the project progresses. However, project teams want enough of the design approved by the project sponsor and technical teams to proceed confidently with the build and test phase activities. Therefore, they combine the concept of creating a minimal viable design with stage gates and proceed to the next phase only after stakeholder approval is received (Figure II.3). Stage gates and incremental approvals help reduce risks for project team members, including the training team. For example, in the design phase, the project sponsor and training manager may agree to provide two deliverables at the end of the design phase:

1. *Training goals and objectives and learning outcomes*: The training design should include approved training goals and objectives and learning outcomes; these elements guide development activities like creating lesson plans.
2. *Subject outline(s)*: The subject outline details the subject sponsor, cost center, prerequisites, training duration, resource description, and so on. It is like a contract between the learners and the instructor.

CYBERSECURITY TRAINING   135

The outputs from the design phase include the minimum viable design from which lesson plans, training content, assessment instruments, and resources can be developed. The training sponsor is the primary approver of the training design document, a significant training milestone.

Microlearning

The design phase of the ADDIE Model of Instructional Design is a creative process supported by extensive online resources (e.g., training design templates) that will reward the learner with design-related content:

- What is the difference between serious games and gamification?
- What are the Universal Design for Learning (UDL) principles?
- How does chunking in learning work?
- How does scaffolding in learning work?
- What are interactive learning best practices?
- What are collaborative learning best practices?
- What is authentic assessment?
- How can I implement the VARK Model?
- Search online for training plan examples.
- Search online for lesson plan examples.

Project Build Phase

The main project activity during the project build phase is to follow the approved design and "build" the product or service. The central project team will follow the design documents and configure the hardware, software, integration, and infrastructure. The technical teams will "build" and test the software in an environment distinct from the "production" environment (where the organization's digital work is performed). Some projects use multiple environments like development, test, stage, and train environments to safely deliver the product or service to their destination: the production environment. Multiple environments improve governance, quality, and risk management. However, each environment requires additional expenditures, such as licensing and maintenance; therefore, the leadership team will weigh the pros and cons when purchasing environments to host project work.

The instructional design project team also has the same approved design when developing training. However, the instructional designer proceeds cautiously since the final product or service the project is creating is not fully approved until UAT is complete and approved by the sponsor. If the instructional design team fully develops the training materials *before* UAT is complete, there is a risk the instructional designers produce training materials that may need to change due to changes made to fix a defect found in testing. The result is some instructional design rework will be required to align the training materials with the UAT-approved system. There may be low-risk work that can be completed before UAT approval, like the initial setup of the LMS and registration process; training workflows may change, but we will still need to configure the registration process.

ADDIE: *Develop Training*

In *Cybersecurity Training*, we take a project-oriented approach to training development. We use a simple work breakdown structure (WBS) to organize training for less involved training development and the requirements traceability matrix when training development is more comprehensive and complex (Figure II.20A). The requirements traceability matrix (Figure II.20B) allows the user to track requirements, logistics or training asset development that have been completed, are in progress, and have not started throughout the project life cycle.

Thus, the instructional design team completes two significant tasks in the ADDIE Develop phase: develop training materials (student and instructor) and finalize training logistics. The WBS or training requirements traceability matrix helps track training activities.

Develop Instructional Strategies

The "develop" phase of the ADDIE process focuses on developing the instructional strategies and the detailed logistics for the instruction.

A

Work Breakdown Structure

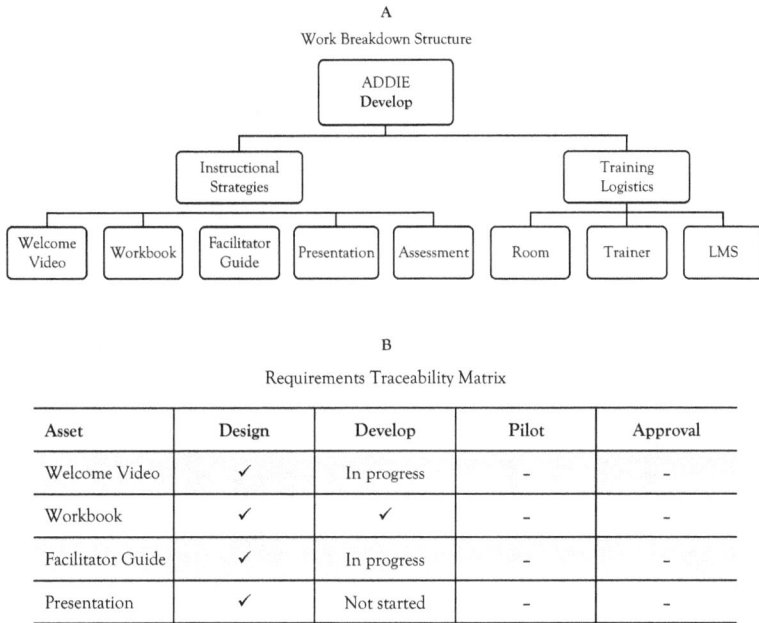

B

Requirements Traceability Matrix

Asset	Design	Develop	Pilot	Approval
Welcome Video	✓	In progress	-	-
Workbook	✓	✓	-	-
Facilitator Guide	✓	In progress	-	-
Presentation	✓	Not started	-	-

Figure II.20 ADDIE Model WBS and requirements traceability matrix

The training development process begins with a draft or high-level outline of the training product, its development, and training product evaluation.

Lesson Plan

A common way to develop valued learning materials is to create a lesson plan guided by training goals, objectives, and learning outcomes. One creates a lesson plan (Table II.6) to guide development activities such as a new specialized course.

The lesson plan can be expanded (and tailored) to include subject and version number, date, subject prerequisites, measures of performance, special instructions/comments, and lesson plan approval details.

When students and instructors see the tight alignment of the training goals and objectives, learning outcomes, and lesson plans, they are more likely to engage in the learning activity, especially when the learner perceives the training as timely, highly practical, or valuable.

Table II.6 Lesson plan example

Lesson plan: introduction to cybersecurity threat detection
Background All IT security specialists benefit from shared knowledge and practices. IT security specialists require the essential knowledge and skills to manage cybersecurity threats. Learners progress through the online self-study module and attend face-to-face training.
Training goal To increase understanding of cybersecurity concepts and practices.
Training objective IT security specialists will understand basic cybersecurity knowledge (e.g., computer networks, privacy, and cybersecurity risk management), including anticipating new threats.
Learning outcomes K0001: Knowledge of computer networking concepts, protocols, and network security methodologies. K0002: Knowledge of risk management processes (e.g., methods for assessing and mitigating risk). K0004: Knowledge of cybersecurity and privacy principles. K0005: Knowledge of cyber threats and vulnerabilities. K0006: Knowledge of specific operational impacts of cybersecurity lapses. K0147: Knowledge of emerging security issues, risks, and vulnerabilities. K0314: Knowledge of industry technologies' potential cybersecurity vulnerabilities. S0357: Skill to anticipate new security threats.
Audience Cybersecurity specialists internal to the organization.
Training mode Flipped classroom (self-study), followed by four hours of face-to-face instructor-led training.
Trainers Trainers are subject matter experts from the IT security leadership and technical teams.

Activities
    1. Review the "Introduction to Security Threat Detection" module.
    2. Complete the assigned readings in the subject's "Resource List."
    3. Complete and pass the precourse online assessment (75% score required).

Assessment Answer the five multiple-choice questions at the end of each section with a minimum pass rate of 80%.
Subject length Pretraining: Eight (8) hours Face-to-face: Four (4) hours

One may develop all the supporting materials or modify existing and freely available online resources (e.g., NICE and NIST organizations have resources for educators and organizations). Consider looking at government websites from other countries for reusable and innovative content.[22] The NIST SP 800-16 *A Role-Based Model for Federal Information Technology/Cybersecurity Training* (2014) offers competency model guidance instructional designers can leverage in cybersecurity awareness and role-based training. For example, cybersecurity awareness training can be strengthened within the cybersecurity learning continuum (Figure I.12). Training and learning are improved when a "program" approach (e.g., the learning continuum) to instructional design, management, and governance is taken.

Instructional strategies can go beyond lecturing; Brown and Green (2016) outline other types of learning activities that have a substantial effect on learning outcome achievement that can be applied to cybersecurity training:

1. Identifying similarities and differences in emerging threat categories.
2. Summarizing and taking notes about a cybersecurity module (e.g., the MITRE ATT&CK framework of adversary methods and tactics).
3. Learning through homework and practice can increase competency, especially for new or challenging cybersecurity knowledge and skills.
4. Nonlinguistic representations (e.g., images, physical sensations like sound and touch, and kinesthetic) can supplement the written text (linguistic representations) in the learning process. For example, cybersecurity response procedures illustrated in a flowchart help the learner understand their CSIRT role in a cybersecurity incident (e.g., "a picture is worth a thousand words").
5. Case studies, short or long, can exemplify cybersecurity best practices.
6. Trainers can use the cooperative learning technique when a team-based approach to learning and working together is the learning modality. For example, a cooperative learning approach can be used in simulation exercises to practice cybersecurity team-based responses to attacks using new cybersecurity SOAR (security orchestration and response) software and their CSIRT playbook. Or the group could develop a one-page infographic to be used in cybersecurity general awareness training.

---

[22] Innovation in licensing is underway (e.g., Creative Commons Licensing), and one is advised to get legal input when using content developed by others.

7. Instructors may collaboratively set learning outcomes with some learners (e.g., board members) to personalize training to achieve unique learning outcomes.

Whatever learning experience is developed, we use and recommend multiple approaches to instruction to accommodate different learning styles (VARK: visual, auditory, reading and writing, and kinesthetic, Figure II.14) and to improve learner engagement.

Most instructional designers decide early whether to develop training materials in-house or purchase commercially available cybersecurity training products and services.[23] Developing training materials is a mini-project and benefits from a project management approach. Instructional designers sometimes break down training materials development into three phases (Table II.7): (1) preproduction, (2) production, and (3) postproduction. These three phases with milestones align with our hybrid project delivery (Figure II.3): (1) initiation, (2) plan, (3) design, (4) build, (5) pilot, (6) implement, and (7) stabilize and closeout. One can add these milestones to the project schedule (Brown and Green 2016).

Table II.7 Training products and services phases and milestones

Phase	Training materials production milestones
Preproduction	Approve scope, budget, schedule, quality, risk, project team, etc.
Production	Develop text/content/storyboards Create a prototype (first draft of the final product or service) for endorsement Create multimedia supporting elements (graphics, audio, video, etc.) Complete an *alpha* version of the working prototype for approval Incorporate feedback in an approved *beta* version of the working prototype Provide a *beta* version to the sponsor/client for approval
Postproduction	Provide training (implement the product or service) Stabilize any outstanding defects Closeout the production and/or project

---

[23] The "make or buy" decision is commonly encountered, and we will not replicate the many useful online resources here in *Cybersecurity Training*. Guidance for the make or buy decision is also well documented in procurement literature.

An online search will return a wide range of training techniques available to instructional designers who want to go beyond the traditional face-to-face teaching method. Innovative approaches exist, including microcredentials, multimodal learning, self-directed learning, interactive software, gamification and serious games, social learning, augmented reality, blended learning, metauniverse mentoring, and so on.

Development Best Practices

Generally, adult learners are engaged when they learn through a problem-solving approach (versus topic-centered instruction). Learning is enhanced when the learner progresses through a series of real-world problems, especially when the instructor is available to provide feedback (e.g., coaching). While some lecturing is helpful, there are other more engaging learning approaches like flipped classrooms, where students come prepared, review the prereading materials, and work in groups on a practical learning activity. The instructor becomes a facilitator in a flipped classroom where the focus is on the learner. Learners who understand "what's in it for me?" engage more in the practical learning activity. Flipped classrooms differ from the traditional approach, where the instructor lectures the entire class and gives assignments to be completed after class and away from the instructor's assistance. In flipped classrooms, the students complete the assigned reading and other learning activities before the class; they come prepared to work on the assignment in the class with the instructor's guidance. The flipped classroom can improve learning.

Instructional designers build in quality by following the best practices of chunking and scaffolding. Chunking is breaking down complex content into manageable and categorized learning modules. For example, the organization may provide training about phishing and passwords, but they will deliver these as two rather than one training module. Chunking can improve learning retention and provide natural breaks in the learning experience.

Scaffolding is related to chunking, where supports are designed into the module to support learning, resulting in learner self-confidence (self-efficacy) and a willingness to try new things. For example, the instructor may discuss phishing and ask learners about their phishing experiences. The instructor may then provide a five-minute lecture with examples of detecting phishing (e.g., problem-based learning). Then, the instructor may provide a short hands-on exercise where students identify phishing and non-phishing threats, earning points on the leaderboard ("pointsification"). Additional scaffolding occurs when the teacher discusses the examples or through Socratic questioning ("what might happen next?"). The instructor may provide student-led scaffolding opportunities (e.g., teach each other as per the Learning Pyramid, Figure II.14) when students form teams for discussions and group work.

We use and recommend gamification and serious games in the learning process; our students like these innovative techniques and, as a result, are more engaged. Gamification is adding game-like elements to the learning process to improve learner engagement. For example, points for learning (pointsification), leaderboards, and small awards (e.g., 3D-printed learning tokens) have been widely used in adult learning. Serious games are games with the primary objective of learning rather than playing the game for entertainment purposes. We use simulations, crossword puzzles, and escape rooms to aid learning. Serious games can be analog or digital. Serious games and gamification techniques are increasingly used in education and training (Lester et al. 2023) and will become staples in the emerging corporate training metaverse.

We configure the learning management systems to distribute mini-formative assessments where students test their knowledge, and the LMS automatically scores the learner's answers. We have used such an approach paired with an LMS leaderboard to gamify engagement and improve learning (Appendix 1, leaderboard use case for formative learning checks through gamification). The formative assessment results are displayed on a leaderboard that the students can see. We can make the learners anonymous using fictitious names on the leaderboard (e.g., Charlie Watts, Karen Carpenter, or Mamady Keita). When 5 to 10 mini-assessments ("test your knowledge games") are used throughout the course, students track their learning and may become more engaged due to friendly competition among the teams or individuals with 3D printed awards for the winners. Research shows that increased learner engagement can lead to improved learning. Therefore, we build into our lessons problem-solving, chunking, scaffolding, gamification, and serious games; we are guided by lesson plans, training goals and objectives, and learning outcomes, all within a project-oriented approach.

While there is a wealth of advice on how to build training materials, Hess and Greer (2016, 270–271) provide e-learning advice:

1. Lessons should be broken down into manageable and cohesive parts.
2. Sequence lessons so learners have background knowledge and skills before moving to advanced content.
3. Multimedia content (e.g., beyond text) should be used to keep engagement high.
4. Words should be presented as audio narration rather than as text when possible.
5. Omit unnecessary information (e.g., align with training goals and objectives and learning outcomes).
6. Connect words and graphics to aid learning.
7. Visuals should be explained through either audio or text but not both.
8. Use conversational language and virtual "coaches" as appropriate.

Instructional designers coordinate with marketing or corporate communications units that may have branding requirements or can provide additional guidance for materials development.

Learning is more likely when students are engaged (Learning Pyramid, Figure II.14). Therefore, seasoned trainers minimize lecturing and design-in engaging activities. While simulations and other learner engagement methods are available, there are also simple techniques to engage learners (Bond University 2022), such as:

- *Predicting the future*: When explaining a concept or process, ask the learners, "what comes next?" The learner must understand the concept (Bloom's comprehension level) and predict what might come next (Bloom's higher levels). Therefore, depending on the content, one can match these engagement methods and questions to Bloom's Taxonomy levels of critical thinking (Figure I.3).

- *Guided reading*: The teacher introduces a concept (e.g., a corporate privacy policy) and provides a focus while the learners are reading the text (e.g., "when you read this data management policy, think about how you manage your data"). Once the reading is complete, the educator guides a group discussion about managing data.

- *Ponderables*: Introduce a problem or question, ask the learners to think about it, and prepare a response. For example, the instructor may ask, "who should be part of our Computer Security Incident Response Team (CSIRT)? Can our business partners provide nontechnical assistance to free up technical resources?" This exercise can be an individual or a group activity. The instructor then engages the learners in a discussion and notes any action items for learner follow-up (e.g., inviting supply chain and finance colleagues to join the CSIRT to improve cybersecurity resilience).

- *Q-Storming*: Set a five-minute time limit and have the teams work on a problem (e.g., what are the central data storage and privacy risks?). The instructor initiates a class discussion.

- *Bookends*: Before introducing a new concept (e.g., hybrid-phishing), inquire about their prior knowledge and experience. Deliver the instruction, and then revisit the original questions.

- *Where do you stand?*: Have the learners stand and ask them a question or pose a controversial statement (e.g., is it possible to prevent all cybersecurity risks?). Have the learners move to a side of the room with others who share the same opinion. Undecided learners can stand in the middle of the room. A group discussion occurs while standing.

- *Take two*: At a natural break in the lesson, have learners work in pairs to identify the most critical concepts. After two or three minutes, have the students report back to the group (avoid repeating the same answers).

- *Burning questions*: With your partner, list any vital question, risk, or problem related to what was learned. These can be discussed when back in the group setting.

- *What if?*: The instructor can pose a hypothetical question to encourage learners to apply the new knowledge or to consider alternative perspectives ("what if you experienced _____ and your supervisor was not available to provide guidance?").
- *De Bono's thinking hats*: The instructor assigns learners "thinking hats" to adopt the associated role. The instructor then poses a question to get the learners thinking from different perspectives. Blue hats manage the exercise (or decision-making process). White hats document facts and list any missing information. Green hats bring creativity and encourage exploring alternatives. Red hats represent feelings and instincts. Yellow hats are optimistic. Black hats advise caution. Blue hats ask each person their input based on the color of their hat.
- *Why should I care?*: Learners work in teams, discuss, and write down why the content is relevant.
- *Beanie catch*: Toss a soft object to a learner who answers your question. The instructor asks another question, and the current student tosses the soft object to another student, and so on.
- *Chain notes*: At strategic points in the lesson, ask students to write a question about the content. At the end of the lesson, students draw a card and answer the question.

All these techniques move away from lectures to improve retention through engagement (see Learning Pyramid, Figure II.14). Many of these techniques also work in team meetings and workshops. For example, "guided reading" can help a group better understand a proposed contract, and "where do you stand exercises" to investigate alternative options during problem-solving.

Cybersecurity Content

NIST special publications like the Security and Privacy Controls for Information Systems and Organizations (NIST SP 800-53, Rev.5, 2020a, 59–64) outline cybersecurity awareness and training content

Awareness and Training Security and Privacy Controls for Information Systems and Organizations	
Literacy Training and Awareness	Specialized Training
Insider Threat	Environmental Controls
Social Engineering and Mining	Physical Security Controls
Suspicious Communications and Anomalous System Behavior	Personally Identifiable Information
Advanced Persistent Threat	Practical Exercises
Cyber Threat Environment	
Practical Exercises	

Figure II.21 NIST awareness and training notional content

(Figure II.21). The content has been arranged into thematic units (e.g., insider threat) to improve learning.

After the content scope is approved, the instructional design team follows the ADDIE Design process to complete design activities. Since it is best practice to tailor and combine (e.g., bring in training requirements from standards, frameworks, and regulations), the training team, sponsor, and cybersecurity specialists determine the specific content to deliver. Since each organization has fluid cybersecurity training and awareness requirements, we avoid detailed recommendations in *Cybersecurity Training* that may work for one organization but not so well for another. We leave it to the reader to select and tailor the appropriate cybersecurity content for their organization.

Develop Assessment Instrument

Instructional designers align assessment and evaluation development with training goals, objectives, learning outcomes, and Bloom's Taxonomy (Figure II.17). They track their development with a training requirements traceability matrix (Figure II.20B). They follow best practices like using multiple-choice and Likert scale questions to assess performance. Their training sponsor approves assessment questions before the instructional designer adds them to the learning management system. They conduct quality control checks on the assessment questions during the pilot study (e.g., determine reliability and validity).

Complete Quality Control Activities

Instructional designers apply quality control principles (find and fix defects) to their training projects. Some revisions to training materials, like updating contact information in a cybersecurity FAQ document, require a simple quality control review (e.g., checking for spelling mistakes). However, when instructional designers develop new cybersecurity training materials where the impact of not learning is high, they follow a more systematic approach to quality control, like using a pilot study to find and fix defects.

Pilot Test Strategy and Plan

A generally accepted quality control best practice is to conduct a pilot study (find and fix defects) of training, evaluation, and logistics before scaling up the training for the rest of the organization. The pilot usually occurs at the end of the ADDIE Develop phase (Figure II.3) and after UAT approval (Figure II.23).

Quality control may range from a simple review, a minor revision to an established training document, to a more formal pilot study (also known as a usability study). Completing a training pilot study is a critical quality control exercise, especially when developing self-directed learning materials that can benefit from a user-centered design approach and critique. A pilot study reveals errors and omissions, evaluates training effectiveness, and collects feedback from the pilot study participants ("learner"). When training includes instructors, invite the instructors to the pilot to ensure that the training materials are usable from the instructor's perspective: "Don't create what we can't deliver!" We have seen an entire project management curriculum of subjects with significant defects due to excluding instructors from the pilot study (and design phase). We apply the Kirkpatrick Evaluation Model to cybersecurity training pilot studies (Figure II.22) and follow best practices. In training pilot studies, instructional designers evaluate reaction and learning; they leave behavior and results evaluation to others (Figure I.4). However, they welcome training feedback from the business units and update training materials using a document version control process.

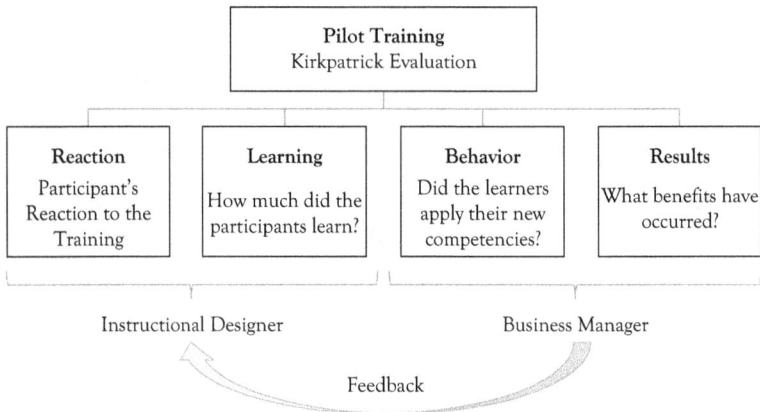

Figure II.22 Pilot study with the Kirkpatrick Model of Evaluation

Conducting a pilot study of new training is like a mini project: instructional designers plan and manage risks with the right stakeholders. Instructional designers take a lean approach to conducting a pilot study that begins with planning:

1. *Plan*: Traditional project management applies here; for example, identify the pilot study scope, approach, schedule, budget, stakeholders, and risks. Identify the stakeholders, trainers, and training sponsor representatives and invite them to participate. The pilot scope is focused on Kirkpatrick's reaction and learning (Figure II.22), leaving learning transfer (behavior) and organizational impact (results) evaluation to others. A planning consideration is the number of pilot study participants. There is a trade-off: the more participants, the more potential for valuable feedback. However, a larger sample size of participants is often more challenging to manage. If more information is desired, the reader is directed to sample size resources from research-related sites.[24] Early during the pilot study, participants review the training goals and objectives,

---

[24] Data collection and sample size considerations have a long history of research and development including this author's work to advance the Delphi method (Skulmoski et al. 2007). We recommend increasing sample size for heterogeneous samples and when results criticality increases.

and learning outcomes; if these are flawed, then what proceeds will likely be defective. The instructional designer continues the pilot test and reviews the subject syllabus in the pilot. Often two types of pilot testing are completed when a comprehensive testing approach is required (e.g., learning criticality is high): (1) review each of the components with the pilot participants and document their feedback, then (2) deliver the subject end-to-end (including pretraining activities) under operational conditions (e.g., register the learners, time the training, use the LMS system in the training room, access learning resources, apply the formative assessments, use the leaderboard, generate learning analytics, etc.). The original training plan baselined in the planning phase accounts for both pilot testing types, which may occur over multiple days or weeks.

2. *Reaction*: There are multiple ways of conducting pilot studies. One way is to have the instructor train and learners engage in the training in the intended training environment (e.g., online or face-to-face learning). The instructional designer introduces the pilot study and proceeds through the lesson plan. Learners and instructors can offer feedback and questions at any point in the lesson. The scope of the feedback can be general (e.g., training room, technology, facilitator guide, handouts, slides, LMS design, etc.) or targeted (e.g., only the assessment instrument). The instructional designer may solicit feedback about the training goals, objectives, learning outcomes, content relevance, and facilitator capability. We conclude by gathering pilot participant feedback about the assessment instrument usability; for example, is the assessment easy to use from both the learner and trainer perspectives? The feedback is incorporated into the next version of the training materials. The training can be repeated, timed, and revised to ensure the training is the appropriate duration.

3. *Learning*: Learning is evaluated using the assessment instrument; for example, to what degree have the learning outcomes (e.g., skills, attitudes, knowledge, etc.) been achieved because of the instruction? Was training successful? To fully assess the learning experience, it is ideal for the instructor to deliver end-to-end training under "live" conditions. In the reaction and learning phases of the pilot, the instructional designer is well suited to conduct the evaluation;

however, in the behavior and results phases, the business manager is better positioned to evaluate their team members' performance and then provide feedback to the instructional designer (Figure II.22).

4. *Behavior*: Evaluating whether the learner successfully applies the new learning (e.g., skills) is crucial. Competency development without application is pointless to the training sponsor. Therefore, the business manager is best suited to evaluate whether the new learning is successfully applied to the job and whether remedial training is required. Evaluating learning transfer is usually out of the scope of the pilot study.

5. *Results*: The business manager assesses whether the learner successfully applies what was learned by analyzing any direct changes to the relevant KPIs (e.g., general awareness training can reduce successful phishing incidents by 20 percent in the next 12 months). Measuring training effectiveness has long been problematic; technological advances and continued integration will result in widespread "measurement of things" (MoT) to benefit training assessment.

Our experience is that evaluation often leads to improvements—a continual improvement approach emphasized in the standards and frameworks detailed in *Cybersecurity Training*. Therefore, our Kirkpatrick Model of Evaluation approach aligns with a continual improvement approach within a project context. When pilot study best practices are used, the training team will likely develop high-quality ADDIE-developed training programs and materials.

Finalize Training Logistics

In the ADDIE Develop phase, instructional designers finalize training logistics (arrange instructors, select classrooms, build the LMS, etc.). They follow a project delivery approach and use standard tools like a WBS and/ or training requirements traceability matrix, project schedule, budget, risk register, and so on to plan, develop, and provide training logistics. They strive for a lean approach and provide the minimum viable training logistics. Since they understand the dependency between training development and user acceptance of training, they do not fully develop and implement all logistics until the sponsor approves the training work package. Therefore, there is a balancing act of too much with too little training development before sponsor approval, the art of risk management.

Microlearning

Pilot studies are a quality control activity: find and fix defects. We are influenced by Shewhart's statistical quality control research (1930s), which influenced Deming to develop his Plan-Do-Check-Act cycle (1950s). The reader may benefit from a deeper understanding of quality management and pilot studies as these techniques can be broadly applied outside of cybersecurity training.

- What is the history of quality control?
- Who was Walter Shewhart, and what were his main achievements?
- What is the purpose of pilot studies?
- What is the pilot study process?
- Can pilot studies be automated?
- What pilot study practices can benefit content creators?
- How are pilot studies conducted in marketing?

Project Test Phase

The project test phase follows the build phase to find and fix defects through the systems testing process (Figure II.23). Testing is a quality control function known as commissioning in construction, pilot testing in training projects, or sound checks and dress rehearsals for entertainment events. In *Cybersecurity Training*, we combine and tailor testing best practices from the PMBOK® Guide, ITIL service management, and ISO quality management. The project team creates a test strategy (high-level approach). The test strategy includes the scope of testing, types of testing to be performed, and how the testing and defect management will be executed (e.g., automated testing). The test strategy and plan include project management information like communications, budget, test team, and the testing schedule. The test plan is more

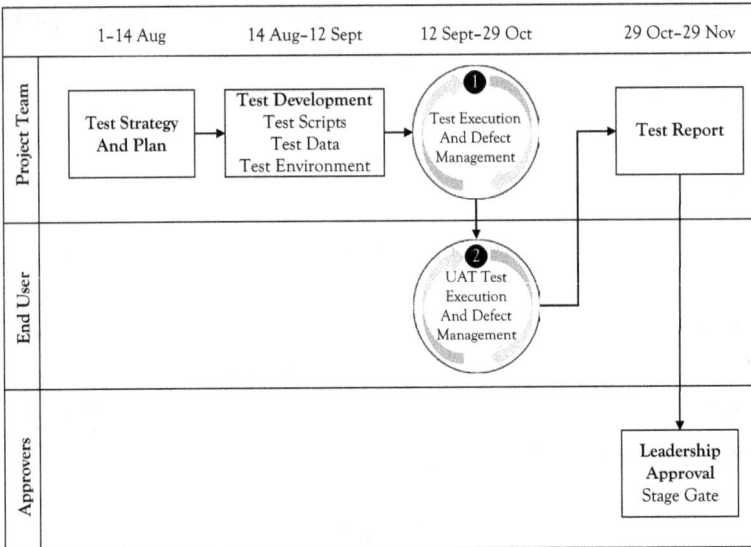

Figure II.23 Systems testing process

detailed and includes a description of the test environment, the test scripts, test data, and test metrics.

When the test strategy is approved, the first round of testing begins with the technical team preparing the test environment, staging the test data, and then executing the test scripts. The technical team finds and fixes any defects away from the project sponsor out of respect for the sponsor's time. Once the system performs as per the approved design, the technical team repeats the testing with the sponsor and/or authorized representatives to achieve "user acceptance" for the product or service (e.g., user acceptance testing) and receives approval to proceed from leadership. Sometimes, a test report is completed and submitted to the sponsor and IT leadership for permission to proceed to the next phase.

Risk Management and Pilot Testing

There is a risk that some of the use cases or functionality might not work and are not provisioned in the go-live version of the new software. Ideally, a change control process keeps the training version of the use cases aligned with the main project. The training team is aware of this risk and may take one of three approaches depending upon the project and sponsor's guidance:

1. *Delay development*: Delay training materials development until most, if not all, functionality, test scripts, and use cases have been tested and approved. This low-risk approach is often used when the use cases or software are complex and innovative.
2. *Incremental development*: The training team can start developing *some* training content when associated workflows and functionality have been tested and approved individually by the end user (e.g., partial approval). The training team must coordinate work with the testing team, who will track testing completion.
3. *Fast track development*: The training team begins training content development before UAT approval or partial approval. The training team can begin development work on the content they deem low risk and unlikely to change (e.g., branding, format, structure, standard workflows, glossary, purpose statements, etc.). Fast-tracking training development is risky but can be used to catch up when the project falls behind schedule. The main risk is content is developed ahead of UAT approval and may need to change because workflows or functionality have changed during the testing process. Fast-tracking is inherently risky.

A common approach is to delay training content development until there is full UAT approval or partial approval, where content is developed iteratively.

Pilot Test Training Resources

When UAT is completed and the sponsor approves the end product or service, an end-to-end pilot test may be executed for training projects. Often, end-to-end pilot testing is focused on the learner and begins with subject advertising and learner registration, through to training following all the lesson plans and learner evaluation (formative, summative, and reactive), through to training record keeping and report generation. The registration process, training, and assessment are timed. Ideally, training during the pilot study is delivered by the trainers motivated to provide valuable feedback (e.g., lessons learned: what worked well? What can be improved?).

Project Transition to Production Phase

The successful test and pilot phases are followed by a T2P phase. The T2P phase is where the last project activities to go-live are completed. It is time to train. The project sponsor informs the organization that a new application is going live or an existing application is being updated. They describe the training and go-live support. The communications include instructions to the end user to raise a service ticket if they encounter any "problems." The ITIL queue manager can categorize the incident as a service request for training assistance, break-fix, or something else. The project sponsor sends the go-live communique to set the organization's expectations for the technology rollout and adoption. The training team will coordinate training with the project manager during detailed go-live planning (e.g., during the T2P phase). The status of training and learning is often part of the go/no-go decision to release the software to the end users.

ADDIE: Implement Training

Training implementation is either the easiest or most challenging phase in the ADDIE Model of Instructional Design process. The training team is more likely to be successful when they tailor and combine best practices (e.g., ADDIE Model of Instructional Design, Kirkpatrick Model of Evaluation, and Bloom's Taxonomy delivered from a project management approach). The training may be as simple as distributing posters about cybersecurity hygiene and free mouse pads detailing phishing avoidance best practices.

Project Training

Two main groups of learners may require training related to the main project: the help/service desk and end users. While the help desk and service desk are terms used interchangeably, the help desk is focused on "break-fix" incidents (e.g., "I can't log in"). In contrast, the service desk is broader and will manage service requests like requests for new laptops, employee onboarding setup, and so on, and provide help desk activities (e.g., "I forgot my password; can you help please?"). Therefore, the help desk may be considered a subset of the service desk. Nonetheless, training is provided to the help or service desk team to understand enough of the application to help end users with basic troubleshooting and perhaps guided by a knowledge base. Their operational goal may be "first contact resolution." The service desk and training teams can work with the vendor to identify the main incidents they are likely to encounter to be included in their training. Indeed, incident management is being transformed by bots and other AI technologies, changing how service and help desk personnel are trained.

The second group of learners that require training is the end user. End users may be a homogeneous or a heterogeneous group of learners. For example, we use the Box Car approach (Figure II.11), where all employees may learn how to use the core workflows of a human resources application, like applying for annual or sick leave. However, only managers and supervisors will receive additional training, including approval workflows for vacation and sick leave requests. Therefore, the Box Car approach allows multiple groups of learners to receive different types of training on the same application in a lean tradition.

The training team follows the training plan, sets up training opportunities, and resources the training with equipment, classrooms, and trainers. They configure the learning management system to allow registration and provide learning resource access to registered learners. Training is delivered according to the curriculum schedule. The LMS may have reporting capabilities that can provide rich analytics about student engagement and learning.

Measuring Project Training Success

The training team measures training success, not by inputs (e.g., training hours or the number of learners who attended training); instead, they measure learning outcomes (Key Performance Indicators—KPIs) like

"80% of the learners will receive 80% or more in the subject evaluation." When the project team achieves the agreed upon "Learning KPI," training may be completed. They may continue to train until everyone registered has received their training, but with the sponsor's agreement, they may close registration for additional training.

The *Cybersecurity Training* authors use output-based metrics to gauge learning success because we avoid the problem where a training vendor delivers the contracted 1,000 hours of training, yet the end users struggle to use the system. Indeed, the vendor may provide double the hours of contracted training, and end users may not achieve the learning outcomes and other KPIs. Therefore, "we don't want training; we want learning!" We tailor and combine best practices, manage risks, build-in quality, and deliver a successful training. We often exceed our stretch KPIs, stay within budget, and complete training on time by following the *Cybersecurity Training: A Pathway to Readiness* approach.

Remedial Training

Remedial training addresses a deficit in knowledge or skills not successfully attained through training. There will likely be learners who do not achieve some learning outcomes during training due to many factors: different learning styles (e.g., a visual versus kinesthetic learner), impeded readiness to learn during the training, multicultural and language differences, environmental conditions (e.g., the classroom was too cold), and psychological barriers (e.g., ADD/ADHD learning conditions). Whatever the reason for the lack of learning, there are many ways to provide remedial training:

- *Repeat subject*: The learner may repeat the entire subject or a component until the desired threshold competence is achieved. However, the subject might not be offered soon, and the subject delivery and training room might not change, resulting in a similar outcome.
- *Mentoring*: Leaders mentor when they work with others to improve their skills and knowledge. Sometimes, a few

minutes of individual instruction can unlock learning so the individual can achieve the desired learning outcome. However, some learning outcomes are more complex, requiring more mentoring effort and formality. The mentor might be someone from the training team or a more senior technical team member. The mentoring may occur immediately upon go-live, where the learner may receive direct support from a mentor or an embedded subject matter expert. Some go-lives have advanced users who provide at-the-shoulder support when new users encounter problems. The supporting person may receive a list of people flagged for potentially benefitting from additional support during the go-live period.

- *Do nothing*: The learner and manager may decide that the competency deficit does not need immediate remediation, and the learner will develop the competency through self-guided learning. The annual performance process may support remediation through formal goal setting.

The learner and supervisor best manage any performance gaps after project training as they are closer to the work than the trainer. However, the training team is supportive and looks for feedback from the operations side to optimize ongoing training (Figure II.22).

Ongoing Training

Remedial training might also be provided by the learner attending regularly scheduled cybersecurity awareness training. Many organizations have an orientation program for new employees where they are introduced to the organization and attend cybersecurity awareness training. Sometimes, training is given when a minimum threshold is reached (e.g., 10 learners). The learner may enroll in the training, and when 10 learners are registered, the learner will be notified of the training date and time. Finally, remedial training can be provided ad hoc or through assistance from a competent co-worker.

Training Optimization

Training is a service, and we strive to improve the value of our services, as do top-tier professionals like you, as evidenced by this book in your hands. Therefore, in *Cybersecurity Training*, we apply quality management principles to the ADDIE Model of Instructional Design. We follow an iterative approach and optimize training through ADDIE Model sprints (Figure II.24). Thus, we follow and recommend an iterative approach to training optimization and apply adaptive project management to our training projects.

Training requirements (e.g., provide new subjects or modules, develop a cybersecurity incident simulation, add more test questions and answers to the test bank, etc.) can be collected and added to the training requirements product backlog (Figure II.24). Like agile project management, the Product Owner—business leadership—can prioritize training requirements. The training team then works on the prioritized training projects and initiatives. For example, Sprint #1 might deliver a new course for Finance to provide information on regulatory changes. Sprint #2 might update a cybersecurity module to add new cybersecurity threats. Finally, Sprint #3 might update all content, assessments, and resources used in the cybersecurity awareness training program to reflect changes to cybersecurity reporting requirements. Recall that the IT department may run concurrently continual improvement projects in addition to ADDIE projects like agile sprints to improve the LMS functionality and Lean Six Sigma projects to streamline the training registration process (Figure I.16). Therefore, many training initiatives (smaller projects) can be managed with an adaptive project management approach with monthly optimization sprints.

ADDIE: Evaluate Training

There are two types of training to evaluate: (1) ongoing cybersecurity training and (2) project-related training. Project training is usually delivered before go-live, so when the new application (e.g., cybersecurity, manufacturing, or finance application) is provisioned to the production

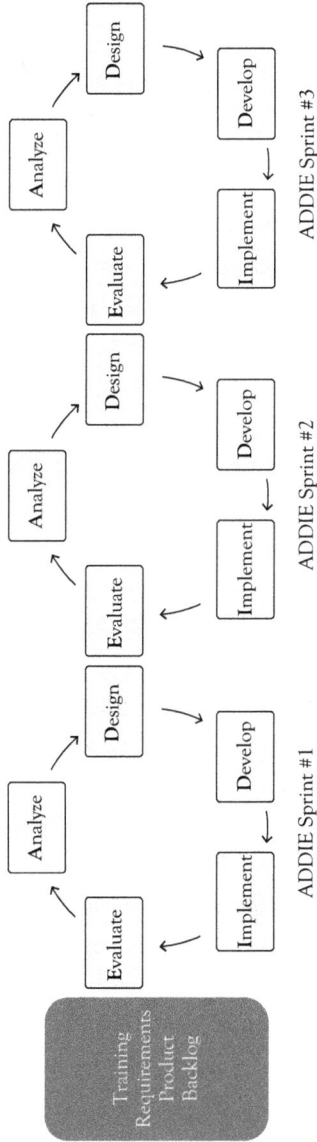

Figure II.24 ADDIE Model optimization sprints

environment, the end users will have sufficient[25] competencies to use the new software. Therefore, training and evaluating learning before the project goes live is a standard best practice.

Project Go-Live: Go/No-Go Decision

The training and learning status (based on preagreed learning KPIs) is a T2P checklist item considered in the go-live decision. Organizations following ITIL may instead use the term "release management checklist" to guide their go/no-go decision. As the project manager and training team complete the T2P action items, they request permission to go-live from the IT department's change authorization board (abbreviated to CAB if ITIL processes are adopted). The CAB's purpose is to keep quality high and risks low. For example, the CAB leadership ensures thorough testing and training are completed, the new application is ready to be integrated into the production environment, sufficient learning has occurred, and the organization (including the IT department) is ready for the new software.

The go/no-go (release) decision criteria should be determined in the planning phase and documented in the project plan with other stage gate criteria. One can also think of the go/no-go decision as the control gates (stage gates) where the project or training manager requests approval to proceed to the next phase (e.g., move from the T2P to the go-live phase). Therefore, they establish measurable and objective criteria for each stage gate to have a shared understanding of the criteria required to proceed to the next phase (e.g., testing results and report have been approved). The project manager develops a concise go-live plan with the release manager, sponsor, and other stakeholders (e.g., the training team), depending on the project and go-live risks. The go-live plan is often based on a template that includes a go-live checklist.

---

[25] How much training and practice to provide is a function of the probability and impact of not learning. For example, the impact of not learning new systems in health care can lead to a sentinel event (e.g., death of a patient), while the impact of not understanding how to use the scheduling feature in a LMS is relatively low, albeit displeasing to those involved in a training scheduling error.

Operational readiness (including competent end users) and IT support readiness are two go-live criteria often evaluated by the CAB. "Readiness" is ambiguous. Therefore, the training team uses metrics to justify organizational readiness, such as "84% of the end-users had an average pass rate of 88% on summative competency assessments. The project sponsor will manage training for the remaining 16% of learners (e.g., mentoring)." Training and other metrics (coordinate with the release manager) can give the CAB insightful readiness decision-making information.

Implement Communications

Project communications management involves the generic process of plan, manage, and monitor communications. The training team considers their stakeholders and roles when planning communications (e.g., Figures II.5 and II.6). They may develop a training communications plan[26] that addresses communications throughout the project, including the final information related to the go-live effort through to project closeout. They monitor training progress and related communications and adjust as required.

Go-Live Communications

The project team may collaborate with the corporate communications unit or others to develop go-live communications. Since it is unlikely that this is the first project to go-live, there may be communications artifacts or templates that can be reused. The training team may participate in two types of go-live communications:

- *Go-live notifications*: Often, the end users are notified in advance of changes and new software through a series of communications. There may be a planned downtime to move the new service into the production environment. When CAB approval is received, the final go-live communication with detailed information and instructions is scheduled for release.

---

[26] Project communications planning is detailed in *Shields Up: Cybersecurity Project Management*.

For example, the date and time of go-live are provided, along with support and additional training information. It is critical to raise service desk tickets related to "system" problems so that a root cause analysis can occur (e.g., is the ticket a training-related or a "break-fix" incident?) and appropriate actions can take place.

- *Scenario communications*: The project manager prepares communications for three scenarios: (1) the go-live is successful, perhaps with a few incidents; (2) the go-live struggled, some experienced problems and the IT team resolved the incidents. The project is proceeding, and the stakeholders are thanked for their patience; and (3) severe technical challenges were faced, and the application is being removed from the production environment. The stakeholders are invited to contact their leadership for more information and to provide recommendations. (Asking for feedback also allows the end user to vent and express their displeasure and concerns. We listen and learn.) These scenario communications are generally out of the scope of the training team; however, they may receive requests for more training if the go-live is challenging due to competency gaps.

Communications can take many forms and offer opportunities to inform the organization of additional training and services your unit can provide. All communications have the potential to return feedback (including training-related feedback), and the training team will try to capture and leverage such feedback as it is a form of assessment and lessons learned. Some organizations require approval for corporatewide communications that may require approvals, advanced planning, and lead time. Branding may concern some organizations that can extend the communications lead time.

Go-Live Support

Some projects establish a command center to support more complex and impactful go-lives. The command center may have the project manager, sponsor or representative, subject matter experts from the business unit (e.g., workflow expertise), infrastructure, integration, IT security, incident queue manager, and so on. When all are in the same room, at least virtually, incidents can be quickly resolved and learning broadly transferred. One may also notify the vendor's technical team at their headquarters of the go-live and request their support for a quick resolution. The project manager encourages the stakeholders to raise incident tickets. The IT team will manage, analyze, and resolve the incidents to make evidence-based decisions regarding project implementation, product or service adoption, and training.

The project team may meet in the command center for a pre-go-live briefing. They may discuss the different scenarios they may encounter and how to manage them. The escalation chain will also be reviewed if an application or service roll-back is required (e.g., remove the new software from the production environment). And there may be pizza, chicken wings, tabouleh, vegetable spring rolls, fruit, and other food to buoy the team and go-live with cake at the end of the week. The command center may remain operational for the first week, and each day may begin with a short stand-up meeting to review the previous day's activities and incidents and to plan for the new day. Leadership news and greetings are often conveyed; indeed, leadership serving ice cream has been known to occur with our servant leaders! The project manager and IT operations leadership monitor the number and nature of incident tickets to determine whether the go-live has more, less, or the average number of incidents for similar past application go-lives. Often, the command center can be shut down when incident numbers are low (e.g., within the pre-agreed quality control limits) and the business is successfully adopting the new application or service.

The training team attends the pre-go-live meeting and the daily stand-ups. During the go-live period, the training team may provide additional or remedial training. The training team may provide at-the-shoulder support by visiting the end users and asking them about the new system. When the trainers are embedded with end users, they are well placed to evaluate learning and to provide technical support and encouragement to nourish the learner's self-efficacy.

Microlearning

With more digital transformation projects, organizations increasingly leverage IT service management frameworks like ITIL and COBIT. You can find more online about these critical go-live best practices that provide a foundation for this book:

- Find go-live communications templates and examples.
- What are ITIL (or COBIT) best practices?
- How does the COBIT maturity model work?
- What are ITIL go-live critical success factors and risks?
- What is the difference between ITIL major, minor, and emergency releases?
- What are the six ITIL approaches for implementing a new software release? The type of release may have training implications, and you will impress your Release Manager with your insight!

Project Go-Live, Stabilize, and Closeout Phase

The day before, during, and after go-live can be highly challenging; however, a comprehensive project management approach aligned to best practices (e.g., risk management, quality management, and technology management) improves the probability of smooth technology delivery and adoption. The project team hands over the project to the IT operations teams, and they provision the new product or service.

Go-Live Training Support and Stabilization

The training team may use the ITIL incident management process and reports to understand any go-live issues (e.g., technical problems, new process adoption problems, training problems, etc.). Indeed, trainers may be one of the incident resolvers in the service desk management system (e.g., a ticket was raised to help an end user with a training-related problem). The training team may review incident tickets for recurring problems or end user service requests that may indicate more profound problems (e.g., inadequate training) or that some end users can benefit from additional support. However, project training may be closed out when the number of service request tickets related to training stabilizes or are within quality control limits.

Learning Project Closeout Activities

The project manager will follow project closeout procedures to terminate the successful project. There may be contracts to closeout, and the procurement team can assist so that the contracts are expeditiously and thoroughly closed out. The requirements traceability matrix is used to track and document deliverables completion to support contract closeout. If training services were contracted, the training team might have a role in verifying the training KPIs. The training team may also participate in a lessons learned exercise, and the training team may complete their internal lessons learned exercise.

Lessons Learned

Lessons learned is a continual improvement activity traditionally conducted at the end of the project. The project manager invites stakeholders to a lessons learned workshop about the completed project. The project manager begins with the agenda and purpose of the lessons learned. The project team values all input and may review workshop facilitation best practices to maximize their effectiveness at drawing out important lessons. Lessons learned workshops open with a general question to trigger participant engagement. "What went well?" and "What can be improved?" are two questions to begin the discussion.

The project manager can also take a focused approach to identify lessons learned about specific aspects of the project. For example, the training manager may ask about the ADDIE Model of Instructional Design used in the project (Figure II.25A). The training manager may ask the instructional designers which ADDIE tools and techniques worked well and can be improved.

Lessons learned about what went well can be captured and improved in each ADDIE Model phase. Or the focus may be on the project

Instructional Design

A

| Analyze | Design | Develop | Implement | Evaluate |

Project Management

B

| Scope | Schedule | Budget | Resources | Risks | Procurement | Communications |

Assessment

C

| Pilot Training | Formative | Summative | Reporting |

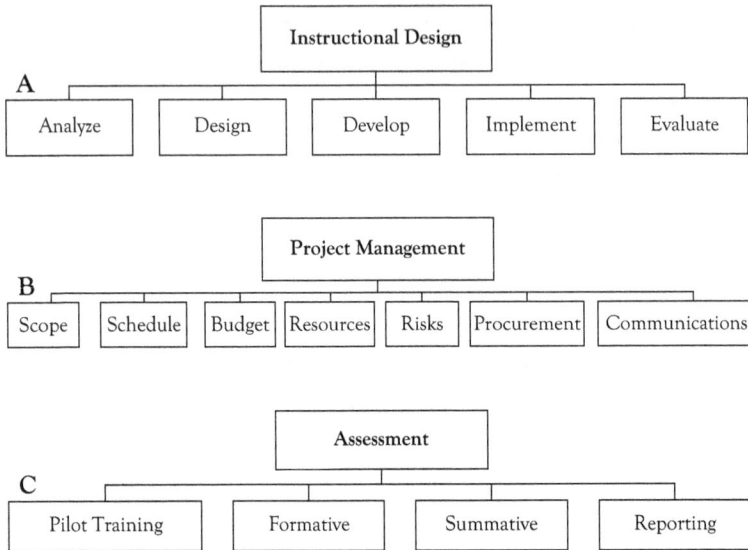

Figure II.25 Training lessons learned: a focused approach

management approach to understand what went well with project communications (Figure II.25B). Or the focus may be on formative and summative evaluation or the quality of training reports (Figure II.25C). As each project is unique, other elements might be analyzed for lessons learned, such as outsourcing success, simulation effectiveness, resource usefulness, and so on. Thus, a focused approach to lessons learned can provide a systematic approach to comprehensively analyze the training project as part of continual improvement efforts.

The project manager may ask a team member to perform the role of scribe so the lessons learned facilitator can focus on drawing out feedback from all workshop participants, and the scribe documents the workshop and its subtleties. Workshops can be recorded for later analysis. If the discussion goes off-track, concepts can be "parked," and the scribe can document any actions for future reference (writing parked feedback with a permanent marker on paper signals the importance of documenting all feedback). These training lessons learned can be provided to the project manager in full or summarized form.

While lessons learned are completed at the end of the project, astute project managers complete lessons learned at the start of each project phase (e.g., test) or ADDIE phase (e.g., design) to leverage the team's previous experiences. When the project manager starts a new phase, they ask the team: "what worked well for you that we can use in this project or phase, and what should we avoid?" The team appreciates such optimization inquiries and feels valued when implementing their ideas. Using lessons learned discussions during the project continues to build teams.

Optimization Requests

The project and training team (Figure II.5) engage with stakeholders (Figure II.6) and collect optimization requests. For example, during the design or testing workshop, an end user may request additional functionality (and training), which may be out of scope as additional integration is required. However, that request and use case may be documented in the closeout report for future action. The closeout report can be started as soon as the project plan is approved and under change control. For example, the project manager starts to populate the closeout report template with basic project information (e.g., mission statement, WBS, high-level Gantt chart, key issues, etc.) and includes any optimization requests as they are raised.

Closeout Report

The closeout report (or a closure report) is usually the final project deliverable and is an evaluation with evidence of project performance. The closeout report template can be shared during the planning phase with the project sponsor and with other relevant stakeholders (e.g., vendors) to manage their expectations and to receive early feedback. A lean closeout template includes:

- *Project closeout checklist*: Closeout checklists provide a lean approach to project closure (like the T2P checklist). The project closeout checklist may be introduced during the project planning phase to manage expectations resulting in lean T2P and closeout phases. Since projects are unique, the project closeout checklist will likely be tailored for each project and may include some of the following for a training project:

o Verify training deliverables acceptance.

o Review training project performance.

o Conduct lessons learned.

o Close down project training resources and off-board team members.

o Project closeout notice to inform stakeholders the project is completed with instructions to access additional training or information.

o Archive project documents and artifacts according to policies and procedures or best practices.

- *Technical report documentation*: Project reports have transformed from text-based to multimedia reports. There are opportunities to "sell" the excellent project work completed, and successful closeout reports have a sales element. Therefore, advanced techniques like storytelling, infographics, multimedia, and other "sales" elements appear in closeout reports, reflecting professionalism and project pride.

- *Basic project information*: Project identifying information like project name, date, scope, rationale, and so on. The training manager can provide similar information for the training project.

- *Project summary*: A high-level project performance evaluation may be included. High-level training results (e.g., KPIs) might also form part of the project summary to substantiate organizational readiness.

- *Scope, budget, and/or schedule performance*: Classical project performance results like comparing actual and planned performance or an advanced analysis like earned value may be included. Any deviances from planned performance targets are explained (e.g., over budget, incomplete scope, early completion, etc.). The requirements traceability matrix is included in an appendix to support the degree of scope completion.

CYBERSECURITY TRAINING 169

- *Resources*: Like project performance, the project and training manager may comment on resource utilization, vendor performance, or procurement if required.
- *Outstanding actions*: A list of outstanding actions for operational teams to complete (e.g., future patching to fix a known defect identified in the test phase). Where possible, the project team raises service tickets with the service desk for each outstanding action with a "to be determined" date with ticket information in the appendix.
- *Signatures*: Stakeholders sign the document to confirm the closeout report's completeness and accuracy (e.g., approve the results, and the project can be terminated).

The project team takes a lean approach to close out the project, keeping quality high and risks low when they follow templates. Vendors and external partners appreciate "clean" project closures with few outstanding actions. The project is closed, IT operations manage the new or updated service, and project participants enjoy a well-deserved break.

Microlearning

Many technology projects have messy endings with project closeout reports that include a list of prioritized "outstanding actions." However, a lean approach to project management and training, based on best practices in frameworks and standards, provides guidance to deliver on time, on budget, and to the approved scope and quality. Our focus in *Cybersecurity Training* is on risk and quality management, resulting in "clean" implementations with few, if any, reported incidents or tickets. Indeed, with front-end-loading, project teams can often deliver and closeout early:

- What are project closeout best practices and risks?
- How can the requirements traceability matrix be used to assist with project closeout?
- What are data management best practices, including long-term archiving?
- What are some project celebration ideas?

ITIL Operations Management and Training

The new application or upgraded service joins the other digital services in the organization's digital ecosystem. The IT department manages its technologies by formally or informally following ITIL service management practices, such as incident management, continual improvement, and workforce and talent management (training). While IT operations manage digital services, the training unit may be involved with ongoing training.

Ongoing Training

Organizations regularly deliver security awareness, cybersecurity training, and specialized training as per the NIST Cybersecurity Framework (Figures I.11 and I.12) in multiple modes, such as self-directed training, simulations, advertisements, and so on. Some advanced specialized training (e.g., for privileged users) may be delivered by the IT security team rather than a human resources department trainer (e.g., train-the-trainer model). Cybersecurity training responsibilities can be negotiated between the IT department and the training unit to ensure the best resource use and training success. Ongoing training is regularly reviewed as part of continual improvement exercises.

Professional Development and Formal Education

Professional development and education in the NIST Cybersecurity Learning Continuum (Figure I.12) are usually managed within the business unit rather than a training unit. Therefore, the training team will unlikely be involved with planning, implementing, and managing professional development or education for the IT team. Instead, professional development and education are managed through the annual performance management process between the manager and the IT professional. When certifications or degrees are achieved, the employee's record in the human resources application can be updated.

Career Development

Recently, the concept of sustainability expanded to career sustainability. Sustainable project-oriented careers are characterized by (1) regular upskilling and (2) networking (Skulmoski et al. 2021). Therefore, we can expect more training activity as the workforce increasingly pursues regular upskilling opportunities. The T-shaped career concept can guide learners to upskill and achieve the right balance for their career goals (Skulmoski 2022). Most IT professionals join an organization, continue taking technical training courses, and earn technical certifications. However, over time, they develop additional nontechnical competencies through short courses or perhaps through a degree program (e.g., an MBA with a project management major). Through time, one can visualize their career development like a T-shape as one progresses through junior technical roles to leadership positions (Figure II.26). Technical competence is represented by the vertical bar. Nontechnical competence is represented by the horizontal bar of the "T" and may include project management, business acumen, leadership, and so on. Therefore, technical teams are encouraged to develop nontechnical skills like project management and for business leaders to develop technical skills like gaining ITIL Foundation certification or skills in data science. To succeed in digital-enabled organizations, people need a broad range of competencies ranging from technical to nontechnical, including project management. Indeed, the pathway to senior leadership is through successful projects.

As digital transformation continues, so does the need for upskilling and training services. Planning your unique T-career is time well spent.

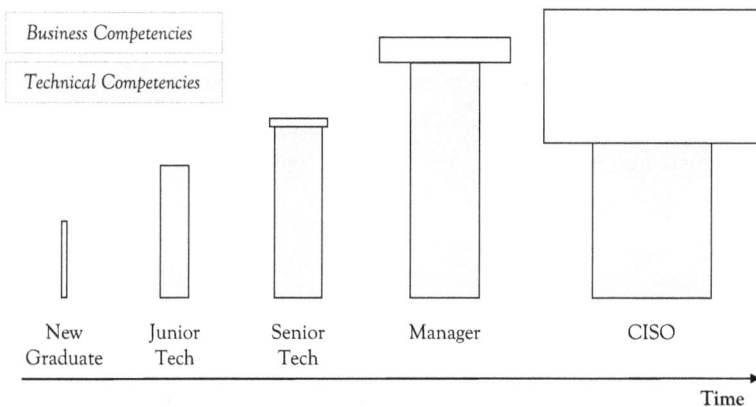

Figure II.26 T-shaped career development

University professors, project managers, consultants, technical specialists, and the instructional design team thrive through continual improvement. As organizations pursue transformation, so does the education sector; expect new ways to learn through innovative partnerships between post-secondary education providers and the corporate world (Ottmann and Skulmoski 2020).

Continual Improvement

We sometimes use continuous and continual improvement in people capacity building, but what is the difference? Continuous improvement involves ongoing improvements. Continual improvement goes further to look externally to benchmark, innovate, and improve. Therefore, in *Cybersecurity Training*, we use "continual improvement," as featured in the ISO 9001 Quality Management standard, since it more closely aligns with our goals and philosophy.

There are many sources of requests for new training, new training applications, simulations, and devices, or changes to training workflows, policies, and procedures. Security policies and procedures are regularly reviewed to determine if organizational changes are required; updated policies and procedures often have knock-on effects, such as the need for training. Business intelligence systems, IT status, incident reports, inter-views with managers, independent observations, evaluation surveys, and IT-led phishing campaigns provide training-related data. Expect expo-nential growth in analytics and reporting capabilities used to justify proj-ects, including training projects.

Continual improvement ranges from micro improvements to initia-tives and projects. People may make micro improvements to a training program, like making a subject description more concise or updating a training template. However, there are more significant and formal contin-ual quality events: major projects and initiatives.

Major Projects

Major projects are usually linked to achieving strategic objectives and often follow the hybrid project delivery approach with tailoring and combining (Figure I.14). The training team participates in the project plan and design phases, developing training materials based on user-approved workflows and functionality (Figure II.3). They train the end users, and the application goes live. Thus, organizations improve through projects, which may have a training component. Organizations also continually improve through smaller projects called initiatives.

Initiatives

Smaller projects, known as initiatives,[27] are used to deliver and optimize training, technology, and processes (Figure I.16). Initiatives require less governance (e.g., documentation) and follow leaner processes. IT departments may use a product backlog to prioritize optimization initiatives. A business operations steering committee may endorse and prioritize initiatives (and projects) in the product backlog. Notice continual improvement's ongoing, iterative, and adaptive nature (Figure II.13); it aligns with best practices in ISO quality management, agile scrum, adaptive project management, ITIL service management, and other standards and frameworks, including cybersecurity.

Therefore, the training team regularly delivers training and participates in and leads optimization initiatives and projects. Cybersecurity threats and vulnerabilities are fluid, resulting in continual learning and training to achieve cybersecurity readiness.

Microlearning

When one reads the professional literature, digital transformation due to AI and quantum technologies will continue for decades. The organizations' quest for continual improvement has resulted in a massive online body of knowledge to guide their efforts:

- For your industry, which is more common: continual or continuous improvement?
- What is a quality improvement quest?

---

[27] Some consider initiatives to be major strategic or transformational projects. We apologize if we add confusion and use the term initiatives for smaller projects that do not require as much governance as larger projects.

- What emerging continual improvement use cases are in your industry and discipline?
- What are ISO 9001 continual improvement best practices and risks?

Conclusion: A Pathway to Readiness

Cybersecurity readiness has become a strategic goal for organizations; their existence is threatened should the organization and its people be ill-prepared to respond and adapt to cybersecurity risks in the current and emerging technical environments (e.g., AI and quantum computing). Therefore, developing, practicing, and adapting cybersecurity readiness is not only an organizational critical success factor but a career critical success factor. What organization does not value employees who can respond and adapt to emerging risks and opportunities? Training and lifelong learning help bring readiness. We began and ended this book by linking training with improved cybersecurity hygiene, contributing to organizational readiness (Figure I.1).

Cybersecurity readiness is like organizational awareness but with a focus on cybersecurity. In *Cybersecurity Training*, we align with global de facto cybersecurity standards and frameworks and tailor our readiness strategies to balance cybersecurity with business objectives. We balance the NIST cybersecurity functions (govern, identify, protect, detect, respond, and recover) and continual improvement efforts with business needs. We wish to avoid unnecessary security constraints on our business partners. We strive for a Goldilocks Approach—just the right amount of cybersecurity balanced with business dexterity. We support CSIRT teams (computer security incident response team) to plan and practice cybersecurity resilience (the ability to recover from attacks and adapt) as part of their commitment to cybersecurity readiness.

Cybersecurity readiness is holistic and involves more than the IT department protecting digital assets. Cybersecurity involves people, processes, and technologies that can be continually improved to achieve and maintain readiness (Figure I.16). Curriculum designers help people develop new competencies through training and professional development. We envision organizations maturing toward ubiquitous learning where learning can occur anytime, anywhere, and just in time to avoid clicking on that deep fake message.

Cybersecurity readiness is everyone's responsibility and is strategically shifting to a business differentiator: digital trust sells. Increasingly, organizations design-in cybersecurity as a matter of necessity. High-performing organizations take an "all hands" approach to cybersecurity; cybersecurity is everyone's job. Since there is room for nontechnical roles in cybersecurity, business partners from finance, supply chain, and risk management are invited to join CSIRT teams to improve resilience (e.g., NIST respond and recovery functions). However, to achieve a holistic approach to cybersecurity readiness, the organization must be engaged in sound cybersecurity practices daily, where leaders are cybersecurity role models.

We have already seen that many cybersecurity incidents are due to human error. The number of people-related cybersecurity incidents will change by the time you read this and may be slightly different for your organization, industry, and discipline. People are a critical weak point in the cybersecurity readiness equation. Nonetheless, organizations can reduce people-related cybersecurity incidents significantly. Cybersecurity awareness and specialized training can provide cybersecurity readiness skills and knowledge to be drawn upon when needed—cybersecurity readiness.

As IT service desk SMEs strive for "first-contact resolution" of issues, the ideal learning environment for some organizations embodies ubiquitous learning. Both approaches aim to help the person progress by removing a problem (e.g., a broken printer) or a knowledge gap (e.g., I do not know what to do now?). The characteristics of ubiquitous learning include (Hwang et al. 2008):

1. *Permanence*: Learning resources for new tasks are always available (e.g., striving to achieve security and privacy goals in a changing environment).
2. *Accessible*: Learners can access all their learning resources, including teachers and experts (e.g., to get detailed information on emerging technology).

3. *Immediate*: There is no lag time to access the training to solve problems (e.g., to get quick advice on handling a potential cybersecurity incident).

4. *Embedded*: Learning is situated in everyday life and work, resulting in contextual learning (e.g., bots are available to assist with new tasks).

Technology advances bring improvements to first-contact resolution targets and ubiquitous learning opportunities. Both are also improved through projects and initiatives!

Readiness is delivered through projects, including cybersecurity training projects. Readiness cannot be purchased from an online store. Therefore, we detailed our project management approach to training, leveraging best practices represented in standards and frameworks. We give you a framework that works for our stakeholders and us. We welcome you to tailor and combine this book to create your unique delivery approach.

Best regards, Chris and Greg.

APPENDIX 1

Leaderboard Use Case

Leaderboards track student progress throughout the learning experience and can improve learner engagement, leading to increased learning. Gamification (adding game-like elements to learning activities) is an engaging training technique that is increasingly used. Leaderboards display the results of learning activities (e.g., formative assessment) and lead to improved learner engagement (especially for learners with a high *achievement motive*).

In our use case, the learner answers five multiple-choice questions about cybersecurity, and their results are anonymously displayed (e.g., our LMS assigns fictitious names to the public leaderboard like Richie Hayward, John Bonham, or Jeff Porcaro). However, each user can view their standing on the leaderboard, as can the instructor. Some LMS include leaderboard functionality, while others push the results to an external (widget) leaderboard (Figure A1.1). You can work with your learning and development team to develop leaderboard functionality for your cybersecurity training to improve engagement.

We expect to see more organizations adopt leaderboards, especially as the metaverse matures, to encourage engagement.

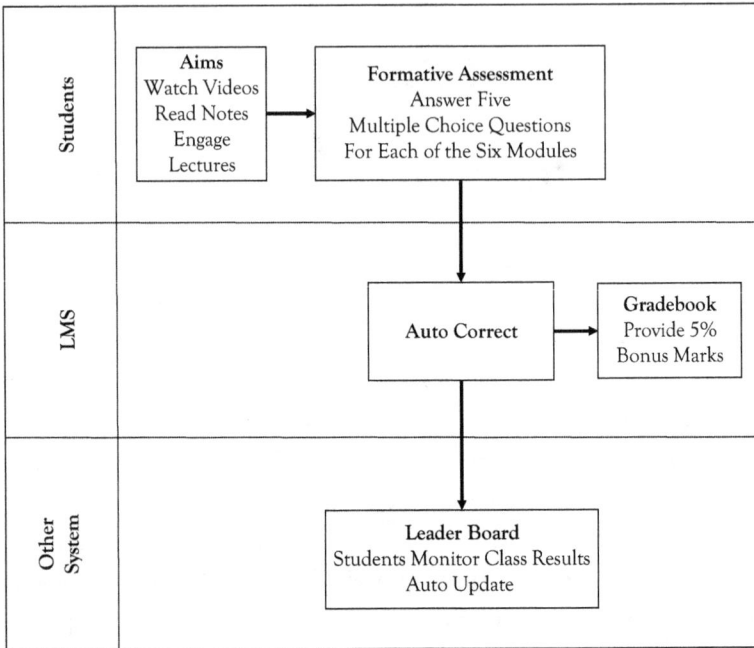

Figure A1.1 Leaderboard use case

APPENDIX 2

Instructional Design Team

While there can be many roles on an instructional design team, there are a few key roles that may be on your training project. Indeed, a single person may be responsible for more than one training role:

Leadership: The instructional design management role directs and monitors the team to implement training aligned with the ADDIE Model of Instructional Design. Since cybersecurity training can be approached from a project management perspective, they apply project management techniques like project resource, risk, and stakeholder management when they work with our instructional design team.

Instructional designer: Experts with deep subject knowledge and experience follow the ADDIE Model to develop content aligned with training goals, objectives, and learning outcomes. Content developers design in best practices from the training and educational technology disciplines. Indeed, many are also trainers.

Trainer: The instructor who delivers training. They may also be involved in the classroom build and may complete formative and summative assessments.

Evaluator: Collects and evaluates training and learning data (formative, summative, reaction, and lessons learned). Since they take a systems approach, the evaluator is involved in most of the learning ecosystem's activities and may also be the instructional designer and trainer.

Learning management system specialist: The LMS application expert can help us with functionality or workflow questions and assistance.

APPENDIX 3

Cybersecurity Roles

The National Initiative for Cybersecurity Careers and Studies (NICCS) is within the Cybersecurity and Infrastructure Security Agency (CISA) and provides tools and resources to advance cybersecurity training and education. The NICCS (2022) has identified 52 cybersecurity work roles aligned with the NICE cybersecurity competency model (Table A3.1).

Table A3.1 **Cybersecurity roles**

All Source-Collection Requirements Evaluation Manager	IT Program Auditor
All Source Analyst	IT Project Manager
Authorizing Official/Designating Representative	Knowledge Manager
COMSEC Manager	Language Analyst
Cyber Crime Investigator	Mission Assessment Specialist
Cyber Defense Analyst	Network Operations Specialist
Cyber Defense Forensics Analyst	Partner Integration Planner
Cyber Defense Incident Responder	Privacy Compliance Manager
Cyber Defense Infrastructure Support Specialist	Product Support Manager
Cyber Instructional Curriculum Developer	Program Manager
Cyber Instructor	Requirements Planner
Cyber Intel Planner	Research and Development Specialist
Cyber Legal Adviser	Secure Software Assessor
Cyber Operations Planner	Security Architect
Cyber Operator	Security Control Assessor
Cyber Policy and Strategy Planner Cyber Workforce Developer and Manager	Software Developer
Data Analyst	System Administrator
Database Administrator	Systems Developer
Enterprise Architect	Systems Security Analyst

(*Continues*)

(Continued)

Executive Cyber Leadership	Target Analyst
Exploitation Analyst	Target Developer
Forensics Analyst	Technical Support Specialist
Information Systems Security Developer	Testing and Evaluation Specialist
Information Systems Security Manager	Vulnerability Analyst
IT Investment/Portfolio Manager	Warnings Analyst

These roles can be combined to fit your unique organization and prioritized for specialized training and resource development (Figure II.10). Then, NICE skills and knowledge recommendations can be developed for role-based training (NICCS 2022).

APPENDIX 4

An Applied Glossary

Our glossary is modified and applied to cybersecurity training. Purists may find we may have tailored our definitions a bit too much. Still, we take some liberty to tailor and combine to create an applied glossary for *Cybersecurity Training: A Pathway to Readiness*.

Adaptive project management: techniques like agile, incrementally build or create the minimum viable product, and are suitable when either the end product or service, or the approach is ambiguous.

ADDIE Model of Instructional Design: a process-based approach to analyze, design, develop, implement, and evaluate training.

Agile project management: an iterative delivery approach using sprints to deliver requirements.

Approval: the authority to allow the project to progress through the phases or to make changes (see Endorsement).

Assessment: the procedure to obtain information about the learner (e.g., data collection).

Best practices: tools and methods considered correct and applicable to most projects and business operations, most of the time.

Bloom's Taxonomy: a way to categorize cognitive thought beginning with knowledge, comprehension, application, analysis, synthesis, and evaluation.

Change Authorization Board (CAB): an IT department board that governs the changes to the production environment (e.g., install patches and updates, implement new applications, etc.). The project manager requires approval to proceed with going live from the CAB.

Chunking: a cognitive process breaking up units into smaller and more manageable pieces, making it easier for the students to process.

COBIT: the Control Objectives for Information Technologies framework provides a governance and management framework to plan, implement, manage, and optimize digital products and services (see ITIL, an alternative framework).

Combine: bring together tools and processes from different standards and frameworks.

Computer Security Incident Response Team (CSIRT): the team comprises technical and nontechnical specialists to respond and recover from cybersecurity incidents. They may follow an incident response and recovery playbook specific to their organization.

Cybersecurity: protecting the organization's information through risk management practices and processes (e.g., prevent, detect, and respond to cybersecurity incidents).

Cybersecurity readiness: the ability of organizations and people to predict and respond to cyber threats and opportunities. Organizations wishing to maintain and improve cybersecurity readiness include continual improvement practices like regular cybersecurity training.

Cybersecurity resilience: the ability of the organization to respond and recover from cybersecurity incidents.

Endorsement: the acceptance of project artifacts (e.g., strategy, scope, schedule, budget, design, etc.) by subject matter experts. Endorsement signals to stakeholders with approval authority that SMEs have completed due diligence and recommend their approval.

Evaluation: the process to determine the success of training and learning (e.g., data analysis). For example, a student received 92 percent on the cybersecurity exam.

Flipped classroom: the learner prepares before the class, and when in the class, the instructor facilitates learning by having the students apply what they have learned to a problem in class with the benefit of immediate feedback from the instructor.

Frameworks: represent best practices but usually exist in the absence of well-defined and globally accepted standards. Frameworks are less prescriptive and more flexible than standards.

Gamification: applying game-like techniques (e.g., awards, pointsi-fication, and leaderboards) to nongame activities to improve engagement. For example, reports can be gamified, where contributors earn points on a leaderboard indicating on-time status updates and other positive project contributions.

Guide to the Project Management Body of Knowledge (PMBOK® Guide): the ANSI standard for project management representing best practices for most projects, most of the time.

Hybrid project management: the traditional or waterfall delivery approach is modified to include adaptive techniques to tailor the project management approach to the specific project. Best practices from external standards and frameworks are combined to arrive at a lean approach to delivering projects and value.

Initiative: a smaller project that requires less governance and supporting documentation. However, project management tools and processes (e.g., risk management) benefit initiatives.

Instruments: physical devices used to collect information (e.g., multiple-choice test). The cybersecurity online, multiple-choice exam through a learning management system is an example of a data collection instrument. Feedback surveys also use data collection instruments.

ISO standards: are guides embodying international best practices agreed upon by experts. They often have a certification pathway indicating meeting the required levels of quality to safely deliver the service or quality for which they are certified.

ITIL: the Information Technology Infrastructure Library is a service management framework of practices that outline how to plan, deliver, operate, and optimize digital services (see COBIT, an alternative framework).

Kirkpatrick Model of Evaluation: a globally recognized method to evaluate training and learning experiences with four levels of evaluation: (1) reaction, (2) learning, (3) application, and (4) organizational impact.

Leaderboard: display results from a learning activity on a device (e.g., a webpage in the learning management system) to engage students to improve their standing by learning.

Learning management system (LMS): a software application with training and learning functionalities, including built-in workflows (use cases), to support organizational learning.

Learning outcomes: describe the specific competencies the learner acquires from the training. Learning outcomes are measurable, and evidence learning occurred.

Measurement: the information collected through the assessment process, like the number of correct responses on the cybersecurity exam.

Metaverse: the next generation of the Internet, integrating the physical and 3D worlds.

NIST Cybersecurity Framework: the American government National Institute of Standards and Technology (NIST) provides a cybersecurity framework of best practices to manage cybersecurity risks.

No-regret project: a cost-effective project under a range of future risk scenarios where value is likely delivered.

Principles: direct how people act in *all* situations. When people adopt principles, they increase the likelihood of a common approach to delivering services and products.

Rubric: an evaluation instrument with performance criteria (measurable and objective) to evaluate the learner's capabilities. For example, an instructional designer can assess a student's penetration test plan (Bloom's Taxonomy: synthesis).

Scaffolding: an instructional strategy where content is broken into smaller units, and learners progress from easy to more challenging concepts with the instructor's assistance, increasing learner self-efficacy (learning and performing confidence).

Serious games: games and simulations with the primary goal of learning rather than having fun.

Servant leader: anyone with the philosophy to serve others so they can succeed, as opposed to traditional leadership based on accumulating power and authority with a top-down orientation.

Simulation: learners practice a skill or procedure in a safe environment under realistic conditions before applying the new competencies to their jobs.

Subject Matter Expert (SME): has deep knowledge and experience in a subject, business area, or technical domain. They may represent the "expert opinion" in the PMBOK® Guide.

Tailor: to bring in and adapt standards, frameworks, techniques, tools, and processes suitable for one's project. In *Cybersecurity Training,* we tailor to adapt within the framework, standard, or method and combine to bring in techniques, tools, and processes from other frameworks, standards, or methods.

Training goals: a general statement about the purpose of the training; the intention of the training.

Training objectives: come from the training goals and are specific statements about what the training program (or instructor) intends to do.

Ubiquitous learning: learning while performing one's work; prompts can guide successful new task completion.

References

Aldag, L., P. Mayer, M. Mossano, R. Duezguen, B. Lofthouse, T. Landesberger, M. Volkamer, and B. Berens. August 10–11, 2020. "An Investigation of Phishing Awareness and Education Over Time: When and How to Best Remind Users." *Proceedings of the Sixteenth Symposium on Usable Privacy and Security, Virtual Conference*. www.researchgate.net/publication/345202653_An_investigation_of_phishing_awareness_and_education_over_time_When_and_how_to_best_remind_users (accessed September 5, 2023).

Allen, M. and R. Sites. 2012. *Leaving Addie for SAM*. 1st ed. Association for Talent Development.

Allen, W.C. 2006. "Overview and Evolution of the ADDIE Training System." *Advances in Developing Human Resources* 8, no. 4, pp. 430–441. https://doi.org/10.1177/1523422306292942 (accessed September 5, 2023).

Alsalamah, A. and C. Callinan. 2022. "The Kirkpatrick Model for Training Evaluation: Bibliometric Analysis after 60 Years (1959–2020)." *Industrial and Commercial Training* 54, no. 1, pp. 36–63. https://doi.org/10.1108/ICT-12-2020-0115 (accessed September 5, 2023).

AXELOS Limited. 2019. *ITIL® Foundation : ITIL 4 edition*. The Stationery Office Ltd.

Bailey, A. n.d. *The Kirkpatrick/Phillips Model for Evaluating Human Resource Development and Training*. Motor Carrier Passenger Council of Canada. www.buscouncil.ca/busgurus/media/pdf/the-kirkpatrick-phillips-evaluation-model-en.pdf (accessed September 5, 2023).

Bond University. 2022. *Interactive Teaching Menu*. Australia: Office of Learning and Teaching.

Brown, A. and T.D. Green. 2016. *The Essentials of Instructional Design: Connecting Fundamental Principles With Process and Practice*. 3rd ed. New York, NY: Routledge.

Cybersecurity and Infrastructure Security Agency (CISA). 2022. "4 Things You Can Do to Keep Yourself Cyber Safe." www.cisa.gov/4-things-you-can-do-keep-yourself-cyber-safe (accessed September 5, 2023).

Forehand, M. 2010. "Bloom's Taxonomy." In *Emerging Perspectives on Learning, Teaching, and Technology*, ed. M. Orey. https://shorturl.at/gtuE4 (accessed September 5, 2023).

Hess, N.A. and K. Greer. 2016. "Designing for Engagement: Using the ADDIE Model to Integrate High-Impact Practices Into an Online Information Literacy Course." *Communications in Information Literacy* 10, no. 2, pp. 264–282.

https://doi.org/10.15760/comminfolit.2016.10.2.27 (accessed September 5, 2023).

Hwang, G., T. Chin-Chung, and S.J.H. Yang. 2008. "Criteria, Strategies and Research Issues of Context-Aware Ubiquitous Learning." *Journal of Educational Technology & Society* 11, no. 2, pp. 81–91. https://ezproxy .bond.edu.au/login?url=https://www-proquest-com.ezproxy.bond.edu.au/ scholarly-journals/criteria-strategies-research-issues-context-aware/docview/ 1437133454/se-2 (accessed September 5, 2023).

IBM. 2022. "Cost of a Data Breach Report 2022." *Cost of a Data Breach Report 2022 Sponsored by IBM* (accessed September 5, 2023).

Kirkpatrick, D.L. 1983. "Four Steps to Measuring Training Effectiveness." *HR Magazine* (Alexandria, Va.) 28, no. 11, pp. 19–25.

Lester, D., G.J. Skulmoski, D.P. Fisher, V. Mehrotra, I. Lim, A. Lang, and J.W.L. Keogh. 2023. "Drivers and Barriers to the Utilisation of Gamification and Game-Based Learning in Universities: A Systematic Review of Educators' Perspectives." *British Journal of Educational Technology* 54, pp. 1748–1770. http://doi.org/10.1111/bjet.13311 (accessed September 5, 2023).

Mat Razali, N.A., K.K. Ishak, M.A.I.M. Fadzli, and N.J.A.M. Saad. 2019. "Cyber Security Education Using Integrative Learning Module for an Optimum Learning Experience." *Advances in Visual Informatics*, pp. 393–403. Cham: Springer International Publishing.

Mayfield, M. 2011. "Creating Training and Development Programs: Using the ADDIE Method." *Development and learning in organizations* 25, no. 3, pp. 19–22.

Microsoft. 2022. "Microsoft Digital Defense Report 2022." *Microsoft Digital Defense Report 2022* | Microsoft Security (accessed September 5, 2023).

Molenda, M. and J.A. Pershing. 2004. "The Strategic Impact Model: An Integrative Approach to Performance Improvement and Instructional Systems Design." *TechTrends* 48, no. 2, pp. 26–33. https://doi.org/10.1007/ BF02762540 (accessed September 5, 2023).

Morrison, G.R., S.J. Ross, J.R. Morrison, and H.K. Kalman. 2019. *Designing Effective Instruction.* 8th ed. New York, NY: John Wiley & Sons.

NICCS: National Initiative for Cybersecurity Careers and Studies. 2022. "The Workforce Framework for Cybersecurity (NICE Framework) Work Roles." *Workforce Framework for Cybersecurity (NICE Framework) | NICCS (cisa.gov)* (accessed September 5, 2023).

NIST. 2003. "Special Publication 800-50: Building an Information Technology Security Awareness and Training Program." https://nvlpubs.nist.gov/ nistpubs/legacy/sp/nistspecialpublication800-50.pdf (accessed September 5, 2023).

NIST. 2014. "Special Publication 800-16, Version 1(3rd Draft): A Role-Based Model for Federal Information Technology/Cybersecurity Training." https://

csrc.nist.gov/publications/detail/sp/800-16/rev-1/draft (accessed September 5, 2023).

NIST. 2018. "Framework for Improving Critical Infrastructure Cybersecurity 1.1." https://doi.org/10.6028/NIST.CSWP.04162018 (accessed September 5, 2023).

NIST. September 2020a. "Special Publication 800-53, Rev. 5: Security and Privacy Controls for Information Systems and Organizations." https://doi.org/10.6028/NIST.SP.800-53r5 (accessed September 5, 2023).

NIST. November 2020b. "Special Publication 800-181, Rev. 1: Workforce Framework for Cybersecurity (NICE Framework)." https://doi.org/10.6028/NIST.SP.800-181r1 (accessed September 5, 2023).

NIST. 2023. "The NIST Cybersecurity Framework 2.0, NIST Cybersecurity White Paper." https://doi.org/10.6028/NIST.CSWP.29.ipd (accessed September 5, 2023).

Office of Cybersecurity, Energy Security, and Emergency Response. 2022. "Cybersecurity Capability Maturity Model (C2M2)." US Department of Energy. www.energy.gov/ceser/cybersecurity-capability-maturity-model-c2m2 (accessed September 5, 2023).

Ottmann, D. and G. Skulmoski. November 22–24, 2020. "Rapid and Responsive Sustainable Careers." *Rapid Cities—Responsive Architectures, Conference Proceedings, American University in Dubai.*

Peterson, C. 2003. "Bringing ADDIE to Life: Instructional Design at Its Best." *Journal of Educational Multimedia and Hypermedia* 12, no. 3, pp. 227–241.

Schwaber, K. and J. Sutherland. 2017. "The Scrum Guide™." *Scrum Guides.* https://scrumguides.org/ (accessed September 5, 2023).

Skulmoski, G.J. and F.T. Hartman. 2000. "The Project's Achilles Heel: Misalignment." *Cost Engineering* 42, no. 12, pp. 33–37.

Skulmoski, G., F. Hartman, and J. Khran. 2007. "The Delphi Method for Graduate Research." *Journal of Information Technology Education* 6, pp. 1–21. http://jite.org/documents/Vol6/JITEv6p001-021Skulmoski212.pdf (accessed September 5, 2023).

Skulmoski, G., C. Langston, A. Patching, and A. Ghanbaripour. 2021. "Sustainable Project-Oriented Careers: A Conceptual Model." In *Research on Project, Programme and Portfolio Management: Integrating Sustainability into Project Management*, eds. R. Cuevas, C.N. Bodea, and P. Torres-Lima. Switzerland: Springer International Publishing.

Skulmoski, G. 2022. *Shields Up: Cybersecurity Project Management.* New York, NY: Business Expert Press.

Stice, J. 2009. *A Refutation of the Percentages Often Associated With Edgar Dale's "Cone of Learning".* Atlanta: American Society for Engineering Education-ASEE. https://shorturl.at/pqINO (accessed September 5, 2023).

Tamkin, P., J. Yarnall, and M. Kerrin. 2002. "Kirkpatrick and Beyond: A Review of Training Evaluation." *The Institute for Employment Studies Report 392, Brighton, UK.* www.employment-studies.co.uk/system/files/resources/files/392.pdf (accessed September 5, 2023).

Tews, T., G. Skulmoski, C. Langston, and A. Patching. September 2020. "Innovation in Project Management Education—Let's Get Serious!," *Construction Economics and Building* 20, no. 3.

Tsunoda, H. and Y. Kino. 2018. "Evaluation of Detailed CSFs and Benefits Model for ITIL Implementation." *International Journal of Innovation, Management and Technology* 9, no. 4, pp. 145–151. https://doi.org/10.18178/ijimt.2018.9.4.804 (accessed September 5, 2023).

van Rooij, S.W. 2010. "Project Management in Instructional Design: ADDIE Is Not Enough." *British Journal of Educational Technology* 41, pp. 852–864. https://doi.org/10.1111/j.1467-8535.2009.00982.x (accessed September 5, 2023).

World Economic Forum. 2022. "The Global Risks Report 2022." *WEF_The_Global_Risks_Report_2022.pdf (weforum.org)* (accessed September 5, 2023).

About the Authors

Gregory J. Skulmoski has had two career paths: an academic and a technology project manager. Greg led pioneering technology projects, including cybersecurity, IoT, Lean Six Sigma process improvement, and auditing/compliance projects. Greg used the tools and processes described in *Cybersecurity Training: A Pathway to Readiness* to win the 2017 Middle East Security Award, CISO Council—100 Rising Stars in Security and Risk (for risk management in technology projects).

Greg was a core member of the PMBOK® Guide 2000 Update Team that revised the original PMI PMBOK® Guide. He is honored to have contributed to other standards such as PMI's Practice Standard for Work Breakdown Structures, Organizational Project Management Maturity Model, and Project Manager Competency Development Framework. Greg participated and contributed to the NIST Cybersecurity Framework v2.0 update project and other global and domestic cybersecurity and quantum technology initiatives. Dr. Skulmoski is a Certified Information Technology Professional and a lifelong Fellow of the British Computer Society.

Therefore, Greg Skulmoski brings both practical experience and a broad theoretical background in project management and cybersecurity, leading to his lean approach to cybersecurity project management. Greg is the author of *Shields Up: Cybersecurity Project Management* with Business Experts Press.

Chris Walker is a Senior Managing Consultant in IBM's EMEA Talent Transformation practice, where he has spent the past 10 years leading technology training and talent development programs. His experience at IBM spans dozens of projects in the UAE, Saudi Arabia, Kuwait, and South Africa. He has led technology training and organizational change management across industries, including health care, telecommunications, automotive, banking, mining, and IT system integration.

Before joining IBM, Chris worked at Kaiser Permanente for 14 years. He led training on numerous business and clinical systems, including leading all clinical systems training for Kaiser Northern California Region's 8-year HealthConnect implementation.

Before his 24-year career in IT implementations and consulting, Chris's early career included 15 years of experience in adult education, including teaching language, music, and yoga and administrating adult education institutions. Chris holds a bachelor's degree in English from Santa Clara University.

Index

Note: Page numbers followed by f and t refers to figures and tables respectively. Page numbers followed by "n" refer to footnotes.

OTHER TITLES IN THE PORTFOLIO AND PROJECT MANAGEMENT COLLECTION

Timothy J. Kloppenborg, Xavier University and
Kam Jugdev, Athabasca University, Editors

- *When Graduation's Over, Learning Begins* by Roger Forsgren
- *Project Control Methods and Best Practices* by Yakubu Olawale
- *Managing Projects With PMBOK 7* by James W. Marion and Tracey Richardson
- *Shields Up* by Gregory J. Skulmoski
- *Greatness in Construction History* by Sherif Hashem
- *The Inner Building Blocks* by Abhishek Rai
- *Project Profitability* by Reginald Tomas Lee
- *Moving the Needle With Lean OKRs* by Bart den Haak
- *Lean Knowledge Management* by Roger Forsgren
- *The MBA Distilled for Project & Program Professionals* by Bradley D. Clark
- *Project Management for Banks* by Dan Bonner
- *Successfully Achieving Strategy Through Effective Portfolio Management* by Frank R. Parth

Concise and Applied Business Books

The Collection listed above is one of 30 business subject collections that Business Expert Press has grown to make BEP a premiere publisher of print and digital books. Our concise and applied books are for...

- Professionals and Practitioners
- Faculty who adopt our books for courses
- Librarians who know that BEP's Digital Libraries are a unique way to offer students ebooks to download, not restricted with any digital rights management
- Executive Training Course Leaders
- Business Seminar Organizers

Business Expert Press books are for anyone who needs to dig deeper on business ideas, goals, and solutions to everyday problems. Whether one print book, one ebook, or buying a digital library of 110 ebooks, we remain the affordable and smart way to be business smart. For more information, please visit www.businessexpertpress.com, or contact sales@businessexpertpress.com.

www.ingramcontent.com/pod-product-compliance
Lightning Source LLC
Chambersburg PA
CBHW061209220326
41599CB00025B/4582